RUSSIA

Oleg Torchinsky

MARSHALL CAVENDISH
New York • London • Sydney

Reference edition published 1994 by
Marshall Cavendish Corporation
2415 Jerusalem Avenue
P.O. Box 587
North Bellmore
New York 11710

© Times Editions Pte Ltd 1994

Originated and designed by
Times Books International, an imprint of
Times Editions Pte Ltd

Printed in Singapore

Library of Congress Cataloging-in-Publication Data:
Torchinsky, O. (Oleg).
    Russia / Oleg Torchinsky. — Reference ed.
      p. cm.—(Cultures Of The World)
    Includes bibliographical references and index.
    ISBN 1-85435-585-6 (set). — ISBN 1-85435-590-2 (vol.)
    1. Russia (Federation)—Juvenile literature [1. Russia
(Federation)] I. Title. II. Series.
DK510.24.T67 1994
947—dc20   93–45927
                      CIP
                      AC

Cultures of the World

Editorial Director	Shirley Hew
Managing Editor	Shova Loh
Editors	Tan Kok Eng
	Roseline Lum
	Michael Spilling
	Winnifred Wong
	Guek-Cheng Pang
	Mikhail Idamkin
	Sue Sismondo
Picture Editor	Mee-Yee Lee
Production	Edmund Lam
Design	Tuck Loong
	Ronn Yeo
	Felicia Wong
	Loo Chuan Ming
Illustrators	Eric Chew
	Lok Kerk Hwang
	William Sim
	Wong Nok Sze
MCC Editorial Director	Evelyn M. Fazio

INTRODUCTION

RUSSIA IS ONE OF THE WORLD'S GREAT POWERS. Not only because its territory is the world's largest, and not because of its huge population, but for the contribution it has made to world history and culture. Russia has a rich and fascinating history as well as a remarkable culture—literature, poetry, music, painting, theater, and cinema—that is known and admired throughout the world.

Russia is also a Eurasian power, and this is reflected in its ancient coat of arms—a double-headed eagle that looks both west and east. The famous English poet Rudyard Kipling once wrote: "East is East, and West is West, and never the twain shall meet." But Russia's example disproves Kipling's words, for it is precisely in Russia's boundless expanses that western and eastern civilizations have converged and mixed, producing a remarkable and original culture.

CONTENTS

Reindeer racing is popular in Russia's frozen north.

CONTENTS

A little Russian girl looks out of her wooden play-house.

GEOGRAPHY

THE RUSSIAN FEDERATION, which covers one-eighth of the world's land area, is the world's largest country, stretching for more than 5,600 miles from east to west, and 2,500 miles from north to south. It occupies most of eastern Europe and almost all of northern Asia. The border between the two great continents—Europe and Asia—runs through its boundless expanses. A monument has been erected where this border is calculated to be; tourists like to be photographed there, standing with one foot in Europe and the other in Asia. Russia's landscape is as varied as the world itself: it includes almost every geographical feature imaginable.

PLAINS AND MOUNTAINS

In the west of Russia there are huge plains stretching thousands of miles that are called the Russian (or East European) Lowland; the Ural Mountains separate this area from another huge lowland—the West Siberian Plain. The southwest of Russia ends in the high ranges of the Caucasus Mountains, where Mount Elbrus (18,465 ft) is the country's highest peak.

In the east of the country is the Central Siberian Plateau, and if you travel farther east you will reach the mountainous regions of southern and northeastern Siberia and the Far East.

Russia is a great marine power. In the north it is washed by the Arctic Ocean and in the east by the Pacific Ocean. Through St. Petersburg it has an outlet to the Baltic Sea, and thus also to the Atlantic Ocean. Russia's ships can reach the Mediterranean through the Black Sea.

Opposite: **A herd of reindeer sweeps across a plain in western Siberia.**

Above: **Sheep cling to a mountainside in Dagestan in the Caucasus Mountains, on the Russian Federation's southernmost border.**

Trading vessels moor on the Volga River at Nizhniy Novgorod, formerly called Gorky, after the city's most famous son, Maxim Gorky, the writer and revolutionary.

RIVERS AND LAKES

Russia has many great rivers. One of the greatest is the Volga River, which is one of Russia's national symbols. Although the Volga is not Russia's longest river, there is no other river about which as many songs and books have been written. The Volga has been known since ancient times, when it was called *Ra;* in the Middle Ages, it was known as *Itil.* Beginning in the depths of Russia as a tiny spring, the Volga flows south, becoming ever wider and stronger. After 2,325 miles it forms a broad delta and flows into the Caspian Sea. A small chapel has been built at the source of the Volga.

But the mighty Volga cannot compete with the huge and powerful rivers of Siberia—the Ob, Lena, Yenisey, and Angara. They are each so wide that if you stand on one bank you cannot see the opposite side.

LAKE BAIKAL Among Russia's thousands of lakes there is one that is unique: Lake Baikal, the world's largest freshwater basin. Its water is so pure and transparent that it is bottled and sold as mineral water. At 5,714 feet, Baikal is the world's deepest lake. It is the habitat of a variety of unusual flora and fauna (1,800 types), including some that are found nowhere else in the world. Another interesting feature distinguishes Baikal from other lakes: 336 rivers flow into the lake, while there is only one outlet, the lower Angara River.

CLIMATE AND SEASONS

Due to its large size, Russia has a variety of different climatic conditions, according to region and the time of year. In the northern arctic and

subarctic zones, the average winter temperature is minus 58°F. By complete contrast, in the south and the Caucasus, summer temperatures can reach 110°F. Western Russia has a typical continental climate of hot summers (up to 86°F) and cold winters (minus 13°F).

The Russian year is clearly divided into four seasons that sharply differ from each other—winter, spring, summer, and fall. The winter months of December, January, and February have frosts, ice, and snowstorms. During this season, the earth is blanketed in white snow and ice. Before the winter comes, birds migrate to warmer lands, insects hide in the tree bark or go underground, and the animals find shelter in dens and lairs.

Spring begins in March and lasts through April and May. This is the time when the first flowers appear from under the snow; they are called snowdrops. The ice on the rivers begins to melt and break up, turning into rivulets of water that run along the streets in the towns and flow onto the meadows and fields in the countryside. Rooks are the first birds to return from faraway countries, announcing the arrival of spring.

Children in a Moscow suburb enjoy playing in the snow during the long winter months.

THE NORTH

The winter is particularly long in the north where the land is washed by the Arctic Ocean. Much of this region is almost perpetually ice-bound. Somewhere in this region of ice and eternal frost is the North Pole.

But the North Pole is not the coldest spot on Earth. The coldest spot is a place called Oymyakon in Siberia. There, the temperature in winter may drop to minus 160°F, a temperature that is hard to imagine. A bird that dares to fly out of its nest in such weather freezes and drops to the ground dead, frozen solid. On such days people stay home, and if they have to go outdoors, they wear clothes made of fur and cover their faces with special fur masks. They have to breathe through cloth or fur to prevent their lungs from freezing.

In the north, the winter lasts seven to eight months of the year. During this period it is dark and cold, with raging snowstorms and blizzards. The boundless deserts are blanketed with snow; the bare forests, the cold and emptiness, are a terrible and unusual sight. But there is a strange phenomenon doctors and psychologists call the "disease of the North." People who have spent some time in the north often want to return there. Neither the warm sea nor palms attract them; all they want is to go back to the cold regions of ice and snow.

One of the most magnificent sights in this part of the world is the Northern lights. The effect of this strange phenomenon is as if someone were showing a color movie across the sky, with gold, white, silvery, bluish, pink, yellow, and red streamers and bands moving in ripples and illuminating the dark winter sky. This enchanting sight lasts one or two hours, gradually fading away until the sky sinks back into darkness. If you are lucky enough to see them, you will never forget the sight. The mechanism that causes this magnificent display is not fully understood, but it is connected with the proximity of the magnetic North Pole to high solar winds.

Opposite, above: **Hares inhabit Russia's central plains and grasslands.**

Opposite, below: **A white polar bear in Russia's northern arctic wastes.**

Spring is followed by the summer months—June, July, and August. Everything blooms, everything thrives and bears fruit.

Fall is considered the most beautiful time of the year—called "golden autumn"—because the forest leaves turn golden-red. Particularly beautiful are the maple trees, whose leaves acquire a golden and bright-red tinge. In November, the trees shed their leaves, with only their bare branches showing a black outline in the forest. The birds migrate southward to warmer lands, and animals hasten to hide in their warm dens.

FAUNA

Thousands of species of animals, birds, reptiles, and insects live in Russia: thousands of different fishes and marine animals inhabit its waters, and thousands of different plants and trees grow in its forests.

The main animals inhabiting the forests of western Russia include the brown bear, wolf, fox, hare, hedgehog, and polecat; and among the most numerous birds are the wood grouse, black grouse, partridge, hazel grouse, crow, magpie, and sparrow.

Other animals include the polar bear, which lives in the north among the snow and ice; the walrus; and the reindeer. Aurochs, a very ancient form of cattle dating back to the Ice Ages, nearly became extinct in recent times. It took conservationists much effort to find several animals and gradually revive the Russian herd. The Siberian *taiga* ("TAI-gah"—subarctic forest) is also the habitat of sables; their fur is so beautiful and soft that it is often called "soft gold." In the Far Eastern *taiga,* there still roam a small number of Siberian tigers, which are an endangered species.

Russia's birds and insect species are much like those found in other regions of the world north of the equator. Many of the birds migrate to southern Asia for the winter months. Russian butterflies are very large but not as bright as their tropical counterparts. Their coloring is designed to blend with the vegetation of Russia's middle belt—its fields, meadows, flowers, and grasses.

FLORA

In Russia forests cover vast areas of land, particularly in Siberia, where forests sometimes stretch for hundreds or thousands of miles. The trees in Russian forests are of the coniferous and deciduous varieties. The coniferous trees include firs, pines, larches, and cedars—all of which are majestic and beautiful trees with needle-like leaves and a wonderful resinous smell. Russians decorate fir trees with glistening ornaments and lights at Christmas time. The deciduous trees growing in Russia include the aspen, oak, maple, poplar, and ash.

Birch trees in winter near Novgorod.

The tree that is particularly loved by Russians is the birch. Its slender branches, smooth white bark, and small bright-green leaves that quiver in the wind have always inspired artists and poets to compare it to a graceful young girl. In pagan times, people paid homage to the birch, decorating it with bright ribbons, flowers, and gifts. The birch was also held in high esteem for other reasons: it made good fuel; its bark could be used for weaving *lapti* (very light and comfortable bark shoes) and also for making special baskets for berries and mushrooms. In ancient times, before paper was invented, the Russians wrote letters, notes, and official documents on birch bark.

CITIES: MOSCOW AND ST. PETERSBURG

Moscow and St. Petersburg are perceived by many Russians as Russia's twin capitals: for many centuries the cities have competed with each other to hold the dominant position as Russia's center.

MOSCOW   Moscow, the officially-recognized capital of the Russian Federation, is one of Russia's oldest cities: it was first mentioned in annals back in 1147. It has played a major role in unifying the Russian lands into a single powerful state. In the 14th century, Moscow was the central point around which the Russian principalities first formed into a unified country. It was in Moscow that the Kievan Grand Duke had his headquarters, which served as a fortress for him and his troops. The town began to grow around the fortress, called the Kremlin. It is interesting to note that the medieval Kremlin fortress remains the political and administrative center of the city and of all of Russia. This is the seat of Russia's government, and where the president receives foreign guests.

The city has developed and grown around the Kremlin and the adjacent massive Red Square, which is Moscow's main square. With a population of around 9 million, Moscow is one of the world's largest cities. It is a large industrial center, with major machine-building and instrument-making plants, steel works, and a large number of factories. It is also a major cultural center with dozens of theaters, cinemas, art galleries, museums, and stadiums.

Modern Moscow consists of glass and concrete high-rise office buildings and hotels similar to those of any other city in the world. The city's residential areas, with their dull looking houses and apartments, are of little interest architecturally. However, Moscow has a great number of historical monuments and fine examples of old churches, palaces, and grand houses of differing styles, which gives the city enormous character.

Moscow cityscape. In the foreground is the Bell Tower of Ivan the Great, built between 1505 and 1508. At 267 feet it is the highest structure in the Kremlin fortress. In contrast, Moscow's many modern apartment blocks can be seen in the background.

ST. PETERSBURG St. Petersburg is a symbol of modern Russia. From 1924 until 1991, it was known as Leningrad, named after Russia's great revolutionary leader, Vladimir Ilyich Lenin. Moscow is a bustling, picturesque city that has developed over the course of centuries, unplanned, with streets clustering together at random. By contrast, St. Petersburg is a European-style city built intentionally according to a particular plan. It is a city of long straight avenues and regularly contoured squares.

On May 16, 1703, Tsar Peter I ordered the city to be built on a site he selected. He conceived this as the new capital of Russia, intending it to play an important role in European life, as well as open a door to the West. He named the city St. Petersburg in honor of his patron saint. The construction of the city was extremely difficult, since it was built on northern marshlands. But Peter employed Europe's and Russia's best architects, and today St. Petersburg is one of the great cities of the world.

St. Petersburg is Russia's second largest industrial and cultural center (after Moscow), and its second, northern capital. Its population now numbers around 5 million. The city has a large number of beautiful historical palaces, squares, and streets. Its magnificent historical sites—the Winter Palace, Dvortsovaya (Palace) Square, the Admiralty, St. Isaac's Cathedral, and the Russian Museum—have been listed by UNESCO as among the greatest treasures of world culture.

Snow thaws around Dvortsovaya Square in St. Petersburg. In the background is the Winter Palace, so called because it was the former winter residence of the Russian tsars. Now it is called the Hermitage Museum and is one of the largest buildings of its kind in the world, with total floor space of 495,000 square feet.

15

Theater Square in Kemerovo, western Siberia.

OTHER REGIONS

There are several other cities and towns of historical significance in western Russia. Among them are Novgorod and Pskov, which before the 16th century were independent city-states ruled by the boyars, as well as Vladimir, Tver, Yaroslavl, Ryazan, Smolensk, and Kostroma.

So far, we have mentioned only the cities of western Russia. Going eastward, there are many other significant towns. For example, the Volga has always been a well settled region, because it provided settlers with fertile land as well as serving as an extremely convenient transportion artery for carrying cargo and people to the north. Nizhniy Novgorod, situated on the Volga, became a major trading center whose fairs won fame worldwide. In the 17th century, a chain of fortresses were built along the Volga River in order to hold back the intrusions of hordes of nomads from the south and east. These fortresses became the towns of Simbirsk (now Ulyanovsk), Samara, Saratov, and Tsarytsin (until recently Stalingrad, but now Volgograd). When invasions no longer threatened, the fortresses turned into prospering commercial centers.

Kazan, a Tatar city and former capital of the Kazan Khannate, stands by itself. Though conquered in the 16th century, it has preserved its Muslim features and is now the capital of Tatarstan.

Beyond the Volga are the vast dry steppes (plains), followed by the Ural Mountains, which are a real treasury of minerals and precious and semi-precious stones, and a major industrial region of Russia. This region began to develop rapidly at the beginning of the 18th century. The cities of this region are Chelyabinsk, Yekaterinburg, Magnitogorsk, and Perm.

Siberia's chief towns are situated in its southern regions along the giant Trans-Siberian railway—Irkutsk, Omsk, Tomsk, and Novosibirsk. These towns were built by rich industrialists. The houses there are strong, warm, and spacious, though not particularly beautiful. These towns have many beautiful palaces and churches, and theaters built in the classical style. Russia's Far East has its own capital cities—Khabarovsk, Vladivostok, and Petropavlovsk-Kamchatskiy. For many years Vladivostok was a secured naval base, and for that reason foreigners were not allowed to visit it. Now it is open to everyone and is becoming a center for Russian-Chinese trade.

A reindeer breeder's camp out on the vast northern tundra.

HISTORY

IN THE TERRITORY of the Russian Federation, Russians account for the bulk of the population. The Russians are Slavs. Slavic peoples are divided into Western, Southern, and Eastern Slavs. The Western Slavs are the Czechs, the Slovaks, and the Poles; the Southern are the Bulgarians, the Serbians, the Croats, and the Slovenes; and the Eastern Slavs are the Russians, the Ukrainians, and the Belorussians. In the first century A.D., the Eastern Slavs lived along the Dnieper River and around Lake Ilmen.

THE SLAVS

The first record of the Slavs has been found in works of fifth and sixth century Byzantine historians. According to these records, the Slavs were a handsome, tall, and strong people with fair hair; they were brave fighting men of great endurance, and hospitable hosts in peacetime. Their main occupation was farming. They sowed rye, wheat, barley, and millet, and traded, hunted, and fished. Beating off forays of aggressive Scandinavian Vikings from the north and nomads from the south, the individual principalities gradually formed a large state that was headed by the grand dukes of Kiev. Kiev, now the capital of Ukraine, was located on the main trade route connecting the Baltic Sea with the Black Sea and the Byzantine Empire.

Kievan Rus established trade with the cities of Asia and Europe—Prague, Constantinople, and Baghdad. In the 10th century, warriors directed by the Kievan dukes Oleg, Igor, and Svyatoslav made raids on the richest and most powerful country at this time—Byzantium. In 911, after Duke Oleg and his large army besieged Constantinople, the Byzantines had to conclude a treaty with Russia, under which Russian merchants received the right to come to Tsargrad (as the Russians called Constantinople) and to trade there free of duty, or tax.

It is mentioned in chronicles that the Kievan Duke Oleg nailed his shield to the gate of the Byzantine capital, Constantinople, as a token of victory.

Opposite: **St. Isaac's Cathedral, central St. Petersburg. The cathedral was named after this saint because St. Isaac's Day is May 30, which is the birth date of Peter the Great, the founder of St. Petersburg. The dome of St. Isaac's Cathedral is 336 feet high and is the third tallest in the world.**

19

A painting by artist Nikolai Roerich (1874–1947) called *Overseas Guests*, depicting Viking traders traveling along the Volga River in the ninth century.

The Russian social system gradually became feudal. As the economy developed, the peasants and craftsmen began to produce more products and goods. Surpluses appeared and the tribal nobility—the elders, military leaders, fighting men—appropriated them. Now they could live at the expense of the work done by peasants and craftsmen who depended on them. The princes seized common lands and gave only small plots to the peasants so that they could maintain themselves and their families by working for the landowners. The feudal lords were called boyars in Rus.

As the old Russian feudal state became larger and stronger, it began to establish diplomatic relations with other European countries. Orthodox Christianity in Byzantium attracted the Russians, as they thought Christianity glorified autocracy. Grand Prince Vladimir I became a Christian in around 988 and made Christianity the official religion in Kievan Rus. The old idols of the heathen gods were thrown into the river. Orthodox priests, who came from Constantinople, christened the Kievans in the water of the Dnieper River.

KIEVAN RUS AND THE MONGOL INVASION

Kievan Rus flourished in the 11th century during the rule of Grand Duke Yaroslav the Wise (1019–1054). Under him, Russia became the largest European state—it stretched from the Gulf of Finland in the northwest, to the Black Sea coast and the lower Danube in the south, and from the Carpathian Mountains in the west, to the upper Volga in the east. Foreign kings sought to establish friendly relations with Rus. Yaroslav married a

Swedish princess, and married his daughters to French, Hungarian, and Norwegian kings.

In the 13th century, a grave trial befell Rus—the powerful Mongol state, with its capital in Karakorum, appeared in the heart of Central Asia. Genghis Khan, a clever, talented, and cruel man, stood at its head. He succeeded in creating an aggressive, well armed, disciplined, and mobile army. Within a short time, the Tatars (as the Mongols were known) had conquered Siberia, China, central Asia, and the Caucasus. Rus was unable to withstand the invasion. In 1223, three uncoordinated Russian detachments were defeated on the banks of the Kalka River (now Kalmius), not far from the mouth of the Don River.

After Genghis Khan's death, the Tatars began their second wave of westward expansion. His grandson, Batu Khan, wanted to conquer the whole of Europe. Over the course of three years (1237–1240), the Russians courageously defended their homeland: many cities were defended to the last man. Only by the end of the 1250s was the rule of the Tatar Khans established in Rus.

Entitled *The Epic Heroes*, this painting by Victor Vasnetsov (1848–1926) portrays the legendary warriors who tried to defend Rus against the overpowering strength of the Tatar hordes.

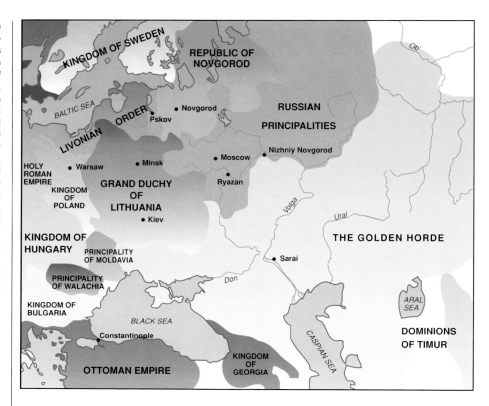

THE RISE OF MOSCOW AND IVAN THE TERRIBLE

On returning from his European raid, Batu Khan and his court settled on the banks of the lower Volga, where the state of the Golden Horde was formed with its capital at Sarai. This foreign oppression brought innumerable calamities to Rus. The destruction of towns and the plundering of the country's riches set Russia's development back two centuries.

The years passed and the country gradually began to recover from the destruction. Towns rose from ruins, becoming the first centers of the struggle for liberation. Moscow grew strong. The city stood out as a great crafts and trading center in an advantageous position: it was at the crossing of trade routes and far from the outlying districts that were constantly threatened by enemy attacks. In the second half of the 14th century, after a leadership struggle, Khan Mamay consolidated the Golden Horde for some time. By then, Moscow had stopped carrying out the Khan's orders, so he decided to punish them. On September 8, 1380, Russians led by

Grande Duke Dmitri Ivanovich met Mamay's army at Kulikovo Field near the Don River. The Russians won the fierce battle. A hundred years later, during the rule of Ivan III (1462–1505), known as Russia's unifier, the Tatar's power came to an end. In 1480, Ivan stopped paying taxes to the Tatars and established Russia's national independence, so Rus became Russia. Under Ivan III's son, Vasily III (1505–1533), all the princedoms and lands of Russia, without exception, were finally unified—some voluntarily, others by force. They formed a new united state, and the wasteful feudal wars ended. The economy and culture began to develop rapidly.

IVAN THE TERRIBLE Under the son of Vasily III, Ivan IV (1533–1584), the state's power continued to grow stronger and some changes occurred within the class of feudal lords. Along with the rich landowners—the boyars—there appeared a social group of small landowners called the gentry. They received land from the boyars in return for military service. This social group was later destined to become Russia's dominant social class.

Under the rule of Ivan IV, the first ruler to be crowned tsar, the Kazan and Astrakhan Khannates were conquered (in 1552 and 1556), and as a result the Volga region became Russian, as did western Siberia and the Urals.

Ivan's reign has gone down in history as one of the most bloody. He instituted a system of terror, *Oprichnina* ("ah-PRICH-ni-na"), directed against both the boyars and the common people. It horrified the whole country. Groups of black-clad *oprichnics* broke into houses, killing and robbing both old and young, and committing other excesses. Because of this he became known as Ivan the Terrible.

Following the death of Ivan the Terrible there was a

Ivan IV, known as "the Terrible." On his head is Monomakh's Cap, the oldest of the tsar's crowns. Legend has it that the crown was given to Vladimir Monomakh, prince of Kiev, by the Byzantine emperor Constantine Monomachus, in the 12th century. But the craftsmanship suggests it was of oriental origin and made in the 13th or 14th centuries.

Tsar Peter I was one of Russia's great reformers. His most far-reaching accomplishment was to draw Russia into the European sphere, which he achieved by transfering the capital to St. Petersburg, and by introducing European ideas and technology. Peter even went so far as to encourage European styles of dress.

period known as the Time of Troubles, when anarchy and instability reigned, one tsar often quickly replacing another. Taking advantage of this, in 1610 the Poles attacked and conquered Moscow. However, the country was saved by a popular movement based in Nizhniy Novgorod and led by Kouzma Minnin, a merchant, and Duke Dmitri Pozharsky, an experienced fighting leader. After several bloody battles Moscow was liberated. In 1613, the Zemsky Sobor (State Council) assembled and elected as the new tsar Mikhail Romanov, who was the first of the dynasty that ruled Russia until 1917.

PETER THE GREAT AND THE 17TH CENTURY

In the course of the next 100 years, the feudal system continued to grow stronger in Russia and serfdom was established. The feudal lands were divided into those of the lord and those of the peasants. The peasant was allotted land; he worked his own plot as well as the landowner's, but he had to work the landowner's ground first, unpaid. He was, in effect, the landowner's slave. Under these terrible conditions peasant riots often broke out.

During this time, towns flourished and crafts developed. Trade also expanded successfully. Caviar, salt, and salted fish were shipped from Astrakhan to other towns; cloth and flax came from Novgorod, Yaroslavl, and Kostroma; leather came from Kazan; and furs from Siberia. Moscow and Nizhniy Novgorod were the largest trade centers. Russia continued to expand its territory into both Siberia and the Far East.

PETER I In 1689, the 17-year-old Tsar Peter (1672–1725) inherited a huge country lagging considerably behind Europe, a result of the 200-year Tatar oppression that had greatly retarded its development. Russia did not have

THE NORTHERN WAR (1700–1721)

In the autumn of 1700, a war broke out against Sweden. It lasted for 21 years and was called the Northern War. The Russian army, badly armed, poorly fed, and badly trained, suffered many setbacks against the talented leadership of the Swedish King Charles XII (1682–1718). Peter decided to reform the Russian army. Some new regiments were formed and trained. Industrial enterprises were built to provide the army with the necessary hardware. There was not enough metal and Peter made a controversial decision: he ordered that church bells be melted into guns, and 300 new guns were cast. The reforms soon yielded results. The Russians won a great victory near Poltava (1709) against the Swedes. Charles was wounded and was nearly taken prisoner. The Nishtadt Treaty (1721) consolidated Russia's victories: it received land along the Baltic Sea coast and so became a European marine power. Following a drawing made by the tsar himself in 1703, the foundations of the Peter and Paul Fortress were laid on the boggy banks of the Neva River. Around this fortress the city-port of St. Petersburg developed, soon to become Russia's new capital.

a developed industry, a modern army or navy, or any convenient sea harbors. The state machinery was old, sluggish, and awkward. It was necessary to look for outlets to the sea as convenient ways for trade and cultural communication with Europe. The country also had to be able to defend itself against Europe's growing military might, and hence create Russia's own modern army and navy.

At that time, the Barents Sea was Russia's only naval outlet. But it was cold and ice-bound for six months of the year, as well as being too far from the center of Russia. The Baltic Sea coasts belonged to Sweden and the Black Sea coasts to Turkey. Russia gained an outlet to the Baltic Sea after extensive territorial gains from the Swedes in the Northern War.

In 1697, a great mission left Moscow and went abroad to make alliances in Europe. The tsar himself traveled incognito, under the name of Peter Mikhailov, a sergeant of the infantry. Under this name he worked as a simple ship's carpenter at a shipyard in Holland. Later, in England, he studied shipbuilding theory and rose to the rank of engineer.

PETER'S REFORMS On his return from Europe, Peter introduced many reforms in Russia: he built metal works so that Russia could produce its own arms (by 1725, there were over 100 factories in Russia); he also started a textile industry. All trade was concentrated in St. Petersburg. A whole

Peter I strongly discouraged the wearing of traditional beards by the gentry and aristocrats and had some of his more stubborn subjects' beards forcibly shaved off! Only the peasants and clergy were allowed to retain their beards, which Peter considered old-fashioned and not European enough.

system of canals connecting the Neva River with the Volga was built in order to make it easier to transport goods from the south of the country to the north.

Peter divided the country into provinces headed by governors. A governor ruled a province and was responsible for tax collection, the armed forces, and public order. The number of officials increased, and a complex bureaucratic machinery was formed to consolidate and maintain the ruling position of the gentry. The estates of the gentry were declared their hereditary property, strengthening the oppression of serfdom. This caused riots and occasional outbreaks of violence in the country.

Peter also introduced new schools; new textbooks on mathmatics, navigation, physics, and chemistry were printed in Russia. He also opened an Academy of Science. All of Peter's reforms helped Russia overcome its industrial and cultural backwardness. As a result, Russia achieved a steep rise in the industrial, scientific, and technical spheres, and became a full-fledged European power.

CATHERINE II

The Russian Empire made great advances during the reign of Catherine II (1729–1796), an epoch often called that of "enlightened absolutism." The clever and educated empress introduced limited freedom of speech, and a liberal press appeared. However, behind the facade of the empress's liberal reasonings about the common welfare, a cruel form of serfdom flourished. A very serious peasant rebellion (1773–1775) led by Emelyan Pugachev swept through Russia during her reign. It was the greatest popular revolt in Europe and shook the empire to its foundation. It involved the whole Volga region. Detachments of rebels conquered a series of towns—Kazan, Samara, Ufa, and Chelyabinsk—and burned

Catherine II reigned in Russia from 1762 to 1796. Though German born Catherine loved her adopted country, and carrying on the work begun by Peter the Great, led Russia into full participation in the political and cultural life of Europe. She gained the throne following a power struggle with her weak and unpopular husband, Tsar Peter III.

down hundreds of landowners' estates. The army suppressed the uprising only with great difficulty.

FOREIGN AFFAIRS As a result of Russian policies in Europe and of the divisions of Poland (1772, 1793, and 1795), Russia received a big part of the Ukrainian and Belorussian lands and a large part of Poland. Following two bloody wars with Turkey (1768–1774 and 1787–1791) the problem of gaining an outlet to the Black Sea was successfully solved, and the Crimean Peninsula and the Sea of Azov became Russian territory. Diplomatic relations with the United States were established: Russia proclaimed the Declaration of Armed Neutrality (1780), supporting the Americans' struggle against England.

THE PATRIOTIC WAR OF 1812

At the beginning of the 19th century, France invaded Russia, led by the Emperor Napoleon Bonaparte. Napoleon made no secret of the fact that he wanted to overwhelm Russia, to subdue and break the country, and distribute its territory among Turkey, Iran, and Poland.

One summer night in 1812, the French army of 640,000 fighting men in three columns crossed over the Neman River near Kovno (now Kaunas in Lithuania) without a declaration of war. Napoleon hoped to overwhelm the Russian army with one decisive blow, occupy Moscow, and dictate his terms. But instead, he found himself involved in a protracted war. The plan of encircling the Russian army failed, and the Russian army regrouped deep in its own territory. Under public pressure the popular Mikhail I. Kutuzov (1745–1813) became commander-in-chief of the Russian army.

An 18th century merchant's house. The merchant class grew steadily under the reforms of Tsar Peter I and Empress Catherine.

27

Field-Marshal Mikhail Kutuzov, commander-in-chief of the Russian army that defeated the French in 1812.

He decided to fight a decisive battle to undermine the French army's strength.

On September 7, 1812, at Borodino field, not far from Moscow, half a million men fought each other in an exceptionally bloody battle. Neither side won decisively, but the Russians retreated and the French captured Moscow.

However, Kutuzov regrouped and strengthened his army, while Russian partisans (guerrillas) harassed French supply lines. The French army began to dwindle, and retreated from Moscow. They suffered terribly from Russian attacks and the cruel winter. Of the 100,000 men in Napoleon's retreating army, only 9,000 managed to return to France.

THE 19TH CENTURY

The war of 1812 brought about a change in the Russian national self-consciousness. The peasants, who had defended their country, returned to a life of slavish servitude under the landowners. The tsarist autocracy introduced *arakcheevschina* (after General Arakcheev, chief councillor to the tsar)—a reactionary policy of merciless serfdom, military drill, and censorial tyranny. Military service, coupled with agricultural service, was required for life: peasant children began to receive military training at the age of seven and at 18 were turned into soldiers. Understandably, these harsh policies caused much resentment.

THE DECEMBRISTS' REVOLT The first secret revolutionary societies appeared, made up chiefly of patriotic young officers and intellectuals. They were later known as the Decembrists because this was the month in which they staged their rebellion. Their aim was to destroy serfdom.

Taking the occasion of Alexander I's (1777–1825) sudden death, the conspiring officers led their soldiers to the Senate Square in St. Petersburg on December 14, 1825. But they hesitated, and were eventually shot down by artillery fire on the orders of Nicholas I (1796–1855), the new tsar.

The revolt on the Senate Square in St. Petersburg, December, 1825, a watercolor painted in 1830 by K. Coelman, depicting the Decembrists' Revolt.

Altogether 579 people were brought to trial, and more than 100 were sentenced to penal servitude and exile in Siberia. Five leaders—P. Pestel, K. Ryleev, S. Muraviev-Apostol, M. Bestuzhev-Ryumin, and P. Kakhovsky—were hanged. But these young conspirators' actions would be emulated many times in the 19th century.

THE CRIMEAN WAR After the suppression of the Decembrists' revolt, the reactionary regime of Nicholas I was established and lasted for over 30 years. He was a rough, cruel man, who dreamed of turning the country into a massive barracks. Even the slightest criticism of the government was punished. Educational establishments were under vigilant supervision, and savage censorship was introduced in literature. Peasant disturbances were mercilessly suppressed. After many years of war, the northern Caucasus region became Russian—with the Chechens, Dagestanis, and other Caucasian peoples losing their independence.

The direct clash of Russian and Turkish interests in their struggle for influence in the Balkan region led to the Crimean War (1853–1856). Russian successes in the opening stages of the war led to England and France joining the war against Russia. Most of the fighting occurred in the Crimea, where a force of over 60,000 English, French, and Turkish troops laid siege the Russian naval base of Sevastopol. For more than 11 months the garrison and the inhabitants repelled enemy attacks, and the allies managed to capture it only at great cost to themselves. After finally defeating Russia, the allies gained a favorable peace settlement, temporarily putting an end to Russia's interests in the Balkans.

ABOLITION OF SERFDOM Losing the war increased opposition to the tsar among the progressive gentry. Peasant disturbances also increased. Under these conditions, Tsar Alexander II (1818–1881), the son of Nicholas I who had died in 1855, said: "It is better to abolish serfdom on the government's initiative than to wait until the masses begin to abolish it by themselves."

Serfdom was abolished on February 19, 1861. The peasants gained their personal freedom—a landowner no longer had the right to buy or sell them. A peasant could get married without the permission of the landowner, could conclude contracts and bargains on his own, and engage in his choice of handicrafts and commerce. The peasants became free citizens with full rights. However, some things did not change:

Troika (1866), a painting by Vasily Perov. Life for the vast majority of Russians was one of back-breaking drudgery in the 19th century. The title is intended ironically, since a troika is usually a vehicle drawn by three horses, not children.

peasants continued to pay a poll tax, and were subject to corporal punishment and military service. In addition, a peasant could leave his village only after paying off all his debts to the landowner, and although the peasants were freed together with the land, the best lands remained in the hands of the landowners. Reforms were also made at the local government level, with the creation of *Zemstvos*— committees responsible for the development of the economy and infrastructure in their region. The law was made more accessible to the majority of people, and schools were opened for the common people.

In the latter half of the 19th century, Russia gradually transformed from a feudal agrarian society to a capitalist industrial power. Food, textiles, and machine-producing industries all flourished. Railroad construction expanded on a massive scale in the period 1860–1890. By the end of the century, the Siberian main line connecting western Russia with the Far East had been completed.

However, peasant rebellions continued because of the limits of the reforms. Secret revolutionary societies appeared everywhere, and it was one of these— *Narodnaya Volya* ("People's Freedom")—that in March 1881 assassinated Tsar Alexander II. Alexander III (1845–1894), the new tsar, established a regime of savage reaction. The leaders of *Narodnaya Volya* were put to death. But workers' disturbances continued, and the first workers' unions were established. In the 1890s, Vladimir Ilyich Lenin (1870–1924) began his revolutionary activities in Russia, and in 1903 founded the Communist Party, the party that later ruled Russia for more than 70 years.

In 1894, a new tsar, Nicholas II (1868–1917), came to the throne.

Nicholas II, the last tsar of Russia, with his wife Tsarina Alexandra, both in ceremonial garb.

THE 1905 REVOLUTION

In Russia, the 20th century began with the unsuccessful war against Japan (1904–1905) for domination in Manchuria, northern China. The Japanese dealt Russia a number of defeats on land and at sea that demonstrated the backwardness of the Russian army, as well as the appalling corruption in the military and state system.

It was dissatisfaction with this war that ignited the events of January 9, 1905. On that day, soldiers fired upon a peaceful demonstration of workers who were marching to the Winter Palace in St. Petersburg with a petition outlining the people's needs. More than 1,000 workers were killed and 5,000 wounded. This savage action provoked a storm of public indignation. On the same evening, the city was covered with a network of barricades erected by the incensed population. Workers disarmed policemen and captured weapons. General strikes occurred in many cities and the peasants revolted in the countryside. A revolt even broke out on board the battleship *Potemkin* in the Black Sea. The peak of the revolution came in December—involving armed revolts in Kharkov, Rostov-on-Don, Sormovo, and Krasnoyarsk. The largest uprising was in Moscow.

For almost two weeks, government forces were unable to suppress the uprising. The government managed to destroy resistance only after using heavy artillery. Savage reprisals were carried out—unions were banned, newspapers and magazines were liquidated, and many revolutionaries and workers were executed.

WORLD WAR I

In the summer of 1914, World War I broke out. Russia, along with Britain and France, was drawn into a vast and protracted war against Germany, Austria-Hungary, and Italy. By 1917, Russia's strength was on the brink of exhaustion. Against a background of industrial disintegration, an aggravated food crisis developed and a feeling of discontent with the government and the unsuccessful war gripped the population. The great losses sustained at the front, economic chaos, and the growing revolutionary crisis at home undermined the morale of the Russian troops. In the tsarist court, Grigory Rasputin (1872–1916), a self-styled "saint," exerted unlimited influence on the tsarina, who believed he could heal her sick son, and in effect ruled the country. Fortunately for Russia, he was murdered by aristocratic army officers in 1916.

THE REVOLUTIONS OF 1917

The year 1917 began with an unprecedented wave of strikes. There were endless demonstrations on the Nevsky Prospekt, St. Petersburg's main thoroughfare, and many clashes with the police. Troops began to support the insurgents, and the city was soon in the hands of the workers and soldiers. The Soviet (Council) of Workers' and Soldiers' Deputies of Petrograd (the new name given to St. Petersburg) was set up.

The *Duma* (state council) established a provisional committee that included representatives of all political parties. On March 15, Nicholas II abdicated. Nicholas and his family were later murdered by Bolshevik revolutionaries in 1918 in Yekaterinburg.

Officially, the country was ruled by the provisional government headed by Prince George Lvov (1861–1925), a famous *Zemstvo* leader. But actually the Petrograd Soviet and other soviets around the country held much of the power.

However, on June 3, 1917, the first All-Russian Congress of Soviets of Workers' and Soldiers' Deputies opened in Petrograd, at which the RSDWP (the abbreviation for the Communist Party) declared its readiness to take power. A month later, on July 3, after armed workers and soldiers tried to seize power, the provisional government went on the offensive. People were arrested and workers' demonstrations were fired upon. The provisional government quickly lost the confidence of the people, since it was unable to end food shortages or the unpopular war with Germany.

On November 7, the revolutionary Red Guard workers, soldiers, and sailors stormed the Winter Palace in St. Petersburg and arrested the

Above: **Alexander Kerensky, a leader of the provisional government established by the State *Duma* in 1917 after Tsar Nicholas' abdication.**

Opposite: **Vladimir Ilyich Lenin, the founder of the Communist Party in Russia, speaks to a crowd in 1917.**

members of the provisional government. There were several reasons for their easy victory. The Communist Party was one of the biggest in the country—it numbered more than 200,000 members at that time, and was well organized, mobile, and had its organizations everywhere—even in the army and navy. For many years, the party had spread its ideas among all sections of the population, and advanced simple slogans that were comprehensible to the masses: "Land—To Those Who Till It," "He Who Does Not Work Shall Not Eat," and so on.

During the first months after the revolution, the new power nationalized land, banks, transportation, and large-scale industry, and established a state monopoly on foreign trade. By signing the disadvantageous, and "revolting" (as Lenin called it) Brest Treaty, Russia ended its war with Germany, and ceded the Baltic regions, part of Ukraine, and Belarus to Germany.

CIVIL WAR There followed a terrible and bloody Civil War (1918–1922), where the Communists ("Reds") and monarchists ("Whites") fought for control of Russia. The Communists eventually triumphed under the

leadership of Lenin and Leon Trotsky (1879–1940). The situation was further complicated by the intervention of foreign powers—Britain, France, Germany, Japan, and the United States—who wanted to restore the old order and hence supported the "Whites."

But most Russian people preferred the "Reds," and it was this grass-roots support that led to an eventual Soviet victory. Leon Trotsky, commander-in-chief, restored discipline and fighting efficiency to the army via draconian methods. The Red Army defeated the "White" generals and their allies one by one. In 1922, the last foreign troops evacuated. The Communists were victorious.

FORMATION OF THE USSR

After the November 1917 Revolution and civil war, the former empire was divided into several independent socialist republics—including the Russian Federation, Ukraine, and Belorussia. After the Civil War, the necessity of their economic and political consolidation became evident. In 1922, representatives of four republics—Russia, Ukraine, Belorussia (now called Belarus), and Transcaucasia (now Georgia, Armenia, and Azerbaijan) signed a declaration forming the Union of Soviet Socialist Republics (USSR). During the 1930s, Kazakhstan, Uzbekistan, Turkmenistan, Kyrgyzstan, and Tajikistan joined the USSR; the Baltic states (Estonia, Latvia, and Lithuania) were annexed by the USSR in 1940 at the beginning of World War II.

In January 1924, Lenin, the founder of the Soviet state and Communist Party, died. An embittered power struggle followed his death, with Joseph Stalin (1879–1953) eventually winning the leadership as general secretary. He was to impose his ruthless dictatorship for the next 30 years.

A huge poster with the faces of the three ideologists upon which Soviet Communism was founded: Karl Marx, Friedrich Engels, and Vladimir Ilyich Lenin. One of Marx's more famous pronouncements was "From each according to his means, to each according to his needs." He envisioned an egalitarian society where everybody was equally provided for, and where the wealthy and strong would support the disadvantaged.

COMMUNISM

Communism is a political and economic doctrine based on the holding of all property in common, actual ownership being ascribed to the community as a whole or to the state. Modern Communism is considered to have been founded by Karl Marx (1818–1883) and Friedrich Engels (1820–1895), with the publication of the *Communist Manifesto* in 1848, and later expounded in more detail in Marx's monumental *Das Capital* (1866–1894).

In the 1920s and 1930s, Lenin's blueprint for modernizing Russia was fulfilled. In the course of industrialization, the modern branches of industry were created and small farms were forcibly collectivized, causing great suffering to the people. All of this was done in the name of Communist ideology. All land became state-owned. With no individual responsibility, agricultural output declined, and the largest country in the world found it could not feed itself and had to buy its grain abroad.

Big improvements were made in education. From 1920 to 1940, almost 50 million men and women became literate. In 1930, universal primary education was introduced. Russia was also the first country in the world to introduce free health care for all its people.

Stalin also imposed a reign of terror in Russia. Books and films were

Right: **Russian troops officially celebrate victory over the Germans at the end of World War II with a parade in Red Square, June 24, 1945.**

Opposite: **Marshal Georgy Zhukov (1896–1974), the commander who launched the successful counter-offensive against the Germans in 1942–1943. Zhukov was a chief member of Stalin's supreme headquarters and figured prominently in the planning and execution of virtually every major engagement in World War II.**

heavily censored, and only those praising Stalin and the Communist Party were allowed. Any opposition to the regime was regarded as a state crime, punishment being imprisonment or death. Purge followed purge, ostensibly in search of counter-revolutionaries and spies—but in fact the fear and suspicion generated was Stalin's way of increasing his hold on power. Watching one's neighbors and reporting to the authorities became a national policy, and arrests were commonplace.

WORLD WAR II

Russia feared invasion when Hitler rose to power in Germany in 1933. One of his many aims was to destroy Communism. Stalin had tried to avoid confrontation with Germany by signing a non-aggression pact with Hitler in 1939, but to no avail. On June 22, 1941, Nazi Germany attacked the USSR. Six months later, German troops occupied half of the west of the Soviet Union, were besieging Leningrad, had been stopped just short of the gates of Moscow, and had reached the Volga in the south. The Germans treated both Russian troops and civilians with appalling cruelty, causing the whole country to rise up and fight the invader.

Financial and military aid was provided by Britain and the United States. The Russians counter-attacked, and a breakthrough was achieved early in 1943 following the five-month Battle of Stalingrad, where 91,000 German troops were captured. The Germans were eventually driven from Russian lands in 1944, and Berlin was captured by Soviet troops on May 1, 1945.

Russian losses, however, were enormous: it is estimated that more than 20 million Russian soldiers and civilians died in World War II.

PERIOD OF RECONSTRUCTION

The postwar period was again followed by government searches for spies and "enemies of the people." Stalin, suspicious of his wartime Western allies, consolidated wartime gains in Eastern Europe and ensured Communist dominance there. An "Iron Curtain" of barbed wire and observation towers was built to segregate Eastern from Western Europe. The nuclear arms race with the United States escalated, consuming enormous resources.

After Stalin died in 1953, there followed a loosening of restrictions under the new general secretary, Nikita Khrushchev (1894–1971). Thousands of innocent people who had been jailed under Stalin were set free. People responded with enthusiasm, and the country made some outstanding achievements—launching the first artificial satellite, the first nuclear power station, and the first man in space, Yuri Gagarin, who became famous throughout the world. Housing was improved, and thousands of families were moved from basements and communal rooms to private apartments. However, Khrushchev's experiments in agriculture led to a further weakening of the economy. In 1964, as a result of internal politics, Khrushchev was removed from power. A period of stagnation followed.

PARTY COLLAPSE

This period was associated with the new general secretary, Leonid Brezhnev (1906–1982). It was a period of superficial prosperity but

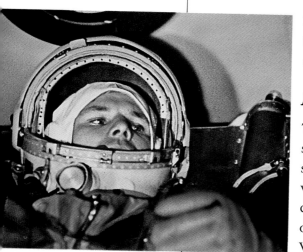

Above: **Yuri Gagarin (1934–1968), Russian cosmonaut who in 1961 became the first man to travel into space.**

Opposite: **Mikhail Gorbachev became leader of the Communist Party in 1985, and quickly ushered in the reforms of *glasnost*, openness, and *perestroika*, restructuring. He was president of the USSR from 1990 to 1991, but with the breakup of the USSR into independent republics, he is no longer in power because each republic has its own leadership.**

38

underlying decay. The economy prospered only because of oil exports; agricultural methods were backward, an ideology nobody believed in prevailed, and culture was virtually destroyed by rigorous censorship. Corruption was common among Party leaders. As time passed, the USSR found itself ruled by a group of old men totally out of touch with the outside world. The disintegration of society was accelerated by the war in Afghanistan, which became a source of national shame for the USSR.

In 1985, the new general secretary, Mikhail S. Gorbachev (b. 1931), tried to save the Party and the country with widespread reforms. He was the first and the last president of the USSR. He did much good, such as stopping the war in Afghanistan; setting many political prisoners free, among them the famous freedom campaigner Andrei Sakharov; and trying to reform the economy and democratize the government. Yet he was hated by the "old guard," Communists who were afraid of losing their power. In August 1991, the reactionaries of the "old guard" attempted to remove Gorbachev and reinstate the old Communist system. The coup was defeated by reform-minded Russians led by Boris Yeltsin. But the unsuccessful coup was fatal for the USSR.

The USSR, a unified and powerful state for so long, disintegrated in December 1991, splitting up into 15 independent countries: the Russian Federation, Lithuania, Latvia, Estonia, Belarus, Ukraine, Moldavia, Kazakhstan, Turkmenistan, Uzbekistan, Kyrgyzstan, Tajikistan, Georgia, Azerbaijan, and Armenia. Today, the various republics loosely cooperate as the Commonwealth of Independent States (CIS).

GOVERNMENT

SINCE THE BREAK-UP OF THE USSR in 1991, the Russian Federation has embarked on a program of reforms that it hopes will bring about greater freedom and democracy. But the path has been and continues to be a difficult one, and many people in Russia are bitter that the once-great Soviet state has been reduced to a state of turmoil.

The political situation in Russia at the end of 1993 was very vague. The prolonged confrontation between the president of the Russian Federation, Boris Yeltsin, and the members of the Supreme Soviet, ended in October 1993 with bloodshed, when troops loyal to the president stormed the Russian parliament building. Yeltsin had dissolved Parliament in order to hold new democratic elections, but hardline members barricaded themselves in and refused to accept the president's decree.

On December 12, 1993, Russia held its first democratic, multi-party elections. No party won a decisive victory in the 450-seat parliament, and

Opposite: **Russian soldiers on leave in St. Petersburg. In 1990, the Soviet army numbered around 4 million, though this number is now much lower with the breakup of the USSR. Many defense industries in Russia are now being converted to civilian use, especially the aviation and space industries.**

Below: **A man waves the Russian flag during the abortive military coup of August 1991. It was due largely to the intervention of Boris Yeltsin, ordinary people, and soldiers that the Communist hardliners failed to regain power in Russia.**

up to eight parties emerged gaining more then 5% of the vote each, with many other candidates gaining individual seats. The result means the three main political groups—the pro-Yeltsin reformists (30%), the Communists (12%), and the nationalists (23%)—and the independent candidates will have to cooperate for any coherent government policy to emerge.

Perhaps the most surprising result of the election was the strong showing of the far-right nationalist Liberal Democratic Party, led by the outspoken Vladimir Zhirinovsky. This party gained 59 seats in the State *Duma*, more than the main pro-Yeltsin party, Russia's Choice. Because of the diverse make-up of Russia's new parliament, much uncertainty remains as to what kinds of policies will be introduced.

POLITICS BEFORE 1991

Before the recent disintegration, the USSR consisted of 15 republics controlled by a centralized federal government and parliament. Each republic had, on a smaller scale, a separate governmental structure much like the one at the federal level. Russia—the Russian Federation—was the largest republic. Each republic was ruled by a local representative body called a soviet. Soviets were the primary elected political organizations consisting of a mixture of peasants', workers', and soldiers' deputies. Since 1977, they had been known as Soviets of People's Deputies.

Any citizen over age 18 could be elected as a people's deputy, and anyone over age 21 could be a people's deputy at the federal

Voters register at a polling station in Kiev, Ukraine. Since 1991, Ukraine has been politically independent from the old USSR, and now holds separate elections. The former countries of the USSR now retain a loose unity under the banner of the Commonwealth of Independent States (CIS), formed in December 1991.

level. The deputies carried out their duties without giving up their permanent jobs and worked on a voluntary basis. If they needed to attend a congress or session, they would be granted paid leave of absence from their jobs. On weekdays, after working hours, their constituents saw them to make requests or voice grievances. Local Soviets were established at country and city level.

The Congress of People's Supreme Soviet of the USSR was the highest body of state authority in the country. These representatives had virtually unlimited power; they could amend the constitution, alter the state's structure, make domestic and foreign policy, and elect the Supreme Soviet and its chairman. The Congress met every year.

The Supreme Soviet was a permanent legislative, administrative, and controlling body of state authority, functioning similarly to a parliament. The members were elected from among the people's deputies by the Congress. The Supreme Soviet consisted of two chambers with equal rights: the Council of the Union and the Council of Nationalities. At their

Red flags displaying the hammer and sickle are brandished in an anti-reform demonstration in Moscow in October 1993. Though many people in Russia are dissatisfied with the hardships that have accompanied the recent liberalization of the economy, those who want to return to the old days of Communist dictatorship are a small minority.

Boris Yeltsin. Born in Yekaterinburg, Yeltsin worked in the construction industry while working his way up through the party ranks at both regional and national level. He was a member of the Supreme Soviet from 1989 to 1991. He became the first president of the Russian Federation in 1991.

joint meetings, they formed the government of the USSR.

In the republics, the highest authority was the Congress of People's Deputies of that republic. The republic's Supreme Soviet was a body accountable to the Congress. The Congress formed the Council of Ministers, who constituted the republic's government. But this complicated, multi-tier governmental structure was no more than a facade. The Communist Party of the Soviet Union (CPSU) was the only ruling party in the USSR, all other parties having been destroyed or outlawed in the 1917 Revolution and ensuing civil war. From the Supreme Soviet down, all positions of authority were held by CPSU members who pursued their party's policy.

The chairman of the USSR Supreme Soviet was the combined head of state and general secretary of the CPSU central committee; for convenience, the foreign press often called him the president. All ministers and trade union leaders were nominated by the CPSU's central committee, the Politburo. Consequently, the CPSU's power was all-embracing, total, and, it seemed at the time, eternal.

Following in this tradition, the general secretary of the CPSU, Mikhail Gorbachev, became the country's first president when the presidency was instituted in the USSR in 1990. This tradition was finally broken in Russia when Boris Yeltsin (b. 1931), a high-ranking official who had withdrawn from the Communist Party, was elected as the Russian Federation's first president in 1991.

A failed coup by reactionary and disaffected leading members of the

CPSU in August 1991 led to the complete collapse of Communist power. The system of soviets was eliminated throughout the country, and replaced by a network of municipal and administrative bodies. The Communist Party is now just one of many parties in Russia competing for popular support.

THE FUTURE

In a referendum held on December 12, 1993, the Russian people narrowly voted to legitimize the new constitution. Under Russia's new constitution Russia is a democratic republic. The president is head of state. The Federal Assembly (parliament), consisting of the Council of the Federation as the upper house, and the State *Duma* as the lower house, has replaced the former Supreme Soviet and is the highest representative and legislative body in the country. The Russian government holds all executive power. The chairman of the government is appointed by the president with the consent of the State *Duma*. Should the State *Duma* decline the president's choice of candidate three times, the president himself has to appoint the chairman of the government, dismiss the State *Duma*, and call for new elections.

As President Boris Yeltsin noted, the results of the referendum and national elections have brought a definite end to the Soviet regime and made an important step toward a new future. However, the results of the parliamentary elections have also shown that Russia's road to democracy and national concord will not be an easy one.

Russia's parliament building, nicknamed the White-house. It was here that Boris Yeltsin rallied support against the coup attempt of August, 1991. It was also the scene of much bloodshed in the confrontation between Yeltsin and the disaffected Parliament on October 4, 1993.

ECONOMY

IN RECENT TIMES, the world and Russian presses have been full of articles analyzing the Russian economy and making forecasts, most of them of a pessimistic nature. Few people dare to say that the situation, although serious, is not so bad.

The Russian economy is suffering great difficulties in converting from a socialist structure to a capitalist-style free market economy. The latter was forcibly destroyed 70 years ago. To understand the Russian economy, it will be worthwhile to briefly outline what happened at that time.

A CENTRALLY PLANNED ECONOMY

After the 1917 Revolution, an attempt was made by the Communists to create an economy based on socialist principles. They believed the capitalist system led to chaotic economic development, cruel exploitation of workers, unemployment, and overproduction crises. Their socialist economy would rest on two basic principles formulated by Karl Marx:

Opposite: **Selling handicrafts at a Sunday market in Moscow. Following the economic and political reforms of the last few years, small businesses and individual entrepreneurs have set up businesses everywhere in Russia.**

Below: **The blast furnace shop at Magnitogorsk Iron and Steel Mill in the Ural Mountains. The Urals are rich in natural resources and hence are one of Russia's major industrial bases.**

A cooperative market in Moscow. The bags being handed out display the colors and emblems of the old Soviet flag and the stars and stripes of the United States flag.

public ownership of the means of production (factories, mines, industry, offices, and agriculture) and a centrally planned economy. One of the first decisions made by the Communists was to nationalize industrial plants and factories and all their equipment, as well as banks and capital.

Later, in 1929–1930, under the process of collectivization, the land became state-owned (state farms) and cooperatively-owned (collective farms). There was no longer any private land ownership. Cattle also belonged to the state. The state became the monopolist in the economy. Centralized planning bodies worked out five-year economic plans. The plans regulated everything from production of aircraft to nails and even eggs.

They believed that since the means of production belonged to the state (and hence, collectively, to the people, because a socialist state is a state belonging to the people), the state should control everything, including planning, financing, and salaries. Under this system, people are supposed to be content and peacefully work for the benefit of society.

The socialist theory assumed that people would work hard because they were working for the collective good, and hence their own good; therefore there would be no reason for them to be lazy or dishonest. Thus, the defects of capitalism—unemployment, financial crises, destructive competition, and so on—would disappear automatically. The five-year economic plans would make it possible to wisely distribute society's resources and to promote development.

THE LIMITS OF A PLANNED ECONOMY However, over the long term, this style of economy seems to have failed. At certain times—for instance, in restoring the national economy after World War I, the Civil War, and World War II—the state's rigid economic monopoly achieved certain successes, but later the basic principles of socialist economic management became an insuperable obstacle blocking economic progress in the Soviet Union and in Russia in particular.

Russian women working on a collective farm near Novgorod.

Abolishing private ownership of businesses and land killed people's desire to succeed or to create and increase their own property. The driving force of personal gain was absent from all work activity. The socialist lifestyle assumed that tireless and selfless labor for the benefit of society (for which the latter paid the worker, though not generously enough) would succeed.

Under this system, there was no reason for the common man, or anyone who was not a fanatical supporter of the socialist ideal, to work hard or to improve or create anything. Everything disappeared into the state's bottomless pocket. A person could work well or badly—either way, he received the same meager wages. Many people were satisfied with this situation. Some did no work for many years, yet were guaranteed their wages or salaries by the state.

Centralized planning also had a ruinous effect: workers and peasants merely had to fulfil the orders passed from above regardless of their practicality. This sometimes resulted in goods being produced that nobody needed and seed being sown into barren or frozen soil. Personal initiative was neither encouraged nor expected.

The party and state elite lived separate lives, and had no understanding of what was going on in the country. They bought goods from their own special shops, visited private medical clinics, spent their vacations in exclusive holiday resorts, and had private planes and trains at their disposal.

As the years passed, the economic situation steadily worsened. For some time, the country lived on "petrodollars" by selling oil and gas at low prices. But that could not last long. Rivalry in the arms race with the United States devoured tremendous wealth; plus a lot of money and energy was spent on supporting "friendly" Communist regimes in Asia, Africa, the Caribbean, and Central and South America.

At the 28th Party Congress in 1991, when the delegates started talking at last about the critical economic situation and the necessity of reforms, it was already too late. The collapse of the Soviet Union in the early 1990s, and the rupture of economic ties between the former Soviet republics that once constituted a single economic whole exacerbated the economic downslide, which rapidly became critical.

A combine harvester at work near Kaliningrad. Though a part of the Russian Federation, Kaliningrad is landlocked by Poland to the south and Lithuania to the east.

THE RUSSIAN ECONOMY IN THE 1990S

In 1992 and 1993, production continued to decline. Economic contacts weakened with other republics of the former Soviet Union. The balance of payments crisis increased. There was a lack of funds, especially hard currency, necessary for purchasing raw materials, accessories, and semi-finished items abroad. As a result of inflation and runaway prices, the purchasing capacity of the population fell and inventories grew.

Significantly, the state catastrophically lost its ability to control the situation at all levels. Oil output sagged; metallurgical production was strangled by the lack of raw materials. The engineering industry continued to slide because of a drop in demand due to high prices. The same situation existed in the chemical industry, oil refining, forestry, and food industries. The production of woolen goods, fabrics, footwear, and foodstuffs also declined.

This process is predicted to continue into 1994. Output is depressingly low for a country of Russia's size and natural resources; but figures indicate that despite the deplorable situation, the economy is alive. Much is being done to stabilize the Russian national currency, the ruble.

Although the situation in Russia is very difficult, there are positive aspects that offer hope for a recovery. The privatization process in different industries is progressing, though with great difficulties and sometimes in the uncivilized, aggressive way typical of periods when capital is first being accumulated. The agricultural industry is waiting for the transference of land to the peasants—a very risky step that could either save the country

An atomic machine-building plant in the Ural Mountains.

51

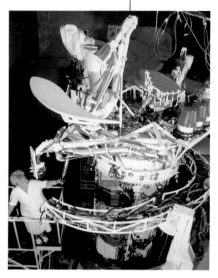

or ruin it completely, depending on the success or failure of this move. Russia must create a successful agricultural base to thrive economically.

AGRICULTURE   As of July 1, 1993, the number of private farms in Russia was 258,100; they occupied a territory of 27 million acres, or 4.7% of farming land and 5.6% of arable land. According to forecasts, by the end of 1993 the number of private farms will reach 340–360,000, and will produce 1.7%–1.8% of total agricultural output.

DEFENSE INDUSTRY   Russia's military-defense industry includes aircraft building, rocket manufacturing, and the space industry. In all of these industries Russia has a major place in the world market. Russia is also a leading arms producer and supplies countries all over the world.

One of the world's most widely used assault rifles, the AK 47 (Kalashnikov), was invented in Russia in 1947. This gun remains the basic weapon of the Russian army and of many other former Communist countries, and versions have been produced in Bulgaria, China, former East Germany, Hungary, North Korea, Poland, and Romania.

AIRCRAFT BUILDING   The Il-86 broad-fuselage passenger liner, produced by the Voronezh aviation plant, is very popular. This is the only series-produced airliner that has never had an accident. On the basis of the successful design of the Il-86, the Il-96-300 airbus has been built. These aircraft

now service the Moscow to New York route, covering the distance of 4,300 miles in nine hours.

NATURAL RESOURCES Another reason that Russia's hopeless economic situation will eventually improve is that the country possesses incalculable natural resources, including oil, coal, gas, metal ores, precious stones, gold, silver, platinum, vast forests, and hydroelectric power.

MANPOWER Finally, the country has immense manpower—people who are able and want to work despite many decades of nearly losing the habit. There can be no doubt that regeneration is not far away.

Russia's labor resources constituted 86.2 million people in 1992, or 58% of the population. In 1993, this number was 85.7 million. The number of people actually employed in the economy in 1992 totaled 72.3 million, or 1.5 million less than in 1991. In 1993, the total number of people employed dropped to about 71 million.

Above: **Fishermen haul in their nets in the Volga River near Astrakhan. Russia's future economic success will depend greatly on the efforts of its vast labor force.**

Opposite, above: **The aerial section of an orbital space communications unit is assembled at the Polyot Industrial Association in Omsk. Russia has built a highly successful space industry.**

Opposite, below: **A recent photo of the now elderly weapons designer, Mikhail Kalashnikov, holding one of the early models of his AK 47 rifle. The initials, AK, stand for Automatic Kalashnikov.**

RUSSIANS

ONE OF RUSSIA'S MOST DISTINCTIVE FEATURES is its multinational ethnic make-up. This originates from the 14th century, with the founding of the Moscow-centered Russian state. Over the next few centuries, because of the rapid outward expansion in Russia, the people of Siberia, the Volga region, the Far East, and the northern Caucasus became a part of the Russian state, with Moscow as their distant focal point.

Sometimes expansion was achieved peacefully, and sometimes by more forceful means. For example, in the 18th century, peaceful conversion of 50,000 Kalmyks was achieved through giving them lands between the river's Volga and Manych in southern Russia, an area they still inhabit today. Throughout history, Christian peoples came to Russia to flee the expansion of the Islamic Ottoman (Turkish) Empire. Greeks, Bulgarians, and Serbs escaped to Russia, trying to avoid Turkish domination. They were accepted and have made significant contributions to Russian culture.

Opposite: **Wearing the traditional long beard of the Russian peasantry, an old Siberian man shows off his faded family snapshots.**

Below: **A Muscovite sells carnations in the street, a favorite flower with many people in the Russian capital.**

THE EMPIRE AS AN ETHNIC MOSAIC

In the 19th century, Russia became a colonial power, but unlike England, France, Holland, and Spain, Russia's colonial expansion was not overseas, but involved swallowing up surrounding territories on the European-Asian landmass. Among these territories were the northern part of the Caucasus,

Right: **The map illustrates how Russia gained its vast empire through the centuries. Russians reached the Pacific coast in the 1640s; their advance across Siberia took less than a century. In the 19th century, Russia set out to solidify its gains by signing treaties with Persia and China and by subjugating the tribesmen of the Caucasus.**

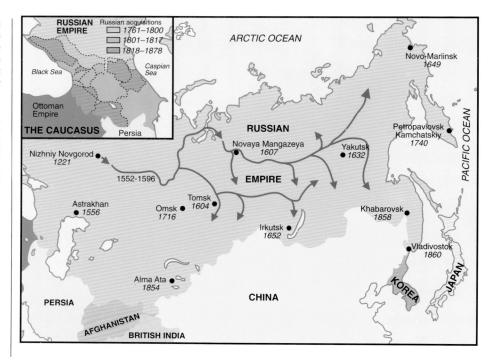

Turkestan (including present-day Uzbekistan), Kyrgyzstan, Tajikistan, and Turkmenistan. They were conquered and exploited by Russia. But in return, Russia offered modern technology and sophisticated European culture to these undeveloped, backward countries. Some highly developed, complex European cultures, such as those of Poland and Finland, were added to the Russian Empire as a result of military conquest.

People from all corners of the empire traveled to the Russian center in order to study and trade and sometimes stayed there, diversifying and enriching Russian life and culture. The Ukrainians, another Slavic people, make up the largest ethnic minority after the Russians and Tatars. Another Slavic people, the Belorussians, make up only a small percentage of the population in the Russian Federation. The process of migration occurred in both directions: many ethnic Russians now live in former Soviet republics like Ukraine, Belarus, Latvia, Lithuania, and Kazakhstan.

From ancient times, various peoples such as Armenians, Georgians, Kazakhs, Uzbeks, and Azerbaijanis lived in Russia. Russia also has populations of Gypsies and Jews. For hundreds of years, many rulers and governments tried to make the Gypsies live in permanent settlements, but to no avail. With the creation of an independent Jewish homeland, many of Russia's Jews emigrated to Israel.

THE SOVIET CITIZEN

In Soviet Russia, the official policy was to create a new type of citizen who no longer identified with a region or republic, but more with the ideology of the party—a "universal" man, dedicated to international socialism. International marriages and migration to other republics were encouraged.

Nowadays, it is evident that this experiment failed. After the disintegration of the USSR, national differences unexpectedly surfaced. Nationalism rapidly increased, especially among the small nations and at the regional level. The many years of suppression of national identities under the Soviet

Catherine II, who was German by birth, invited families from Germany to settle in Russia, and after some time a large German colony formed near Saratov on the Volga River. After the revolution of 1917, this was transformed into the Volga District German Republic, but this republic broke up during World War II because of the Nazi invasion and has not since been revived.

A mother and child from Pskov, one of Russia's oldest cities.

regime led to a massive explosion of nationalist feeling in all parts of the former USSR. Sporadic local wars flared up in many of the distant outposts of the former Soviet Union, particularly in the northern Caucasus, Armenia, Azerbaijan, the Baltic states, and Moldavia.

ETHNIC DIVERSITY

There are now more than 100 nationalities living in Russia. According to 1993 forecasts, the population is 148.7 million, of which 80% are Russians.

But in truth the Russians are not a homogeneous group but originate from a variety of backgrounds. Russians living in the north—in Murmansk and Archangelsk—or in Siberia, or in the areas bordering upon Ukraine, are significantly different from each other in their customs and attitudes. Russia's enormous size makes such variations inevitable between people thousands of miles apart.

The modern Russians bearing the closest resemblance to their Slavic ancestors are probably those who live just north of Moscow—the inhabitants of Pskov, Archangelsk, and Novgorod. They are fair-haired and blue-eyed, with lean, narrow faces. Asian features are not common in this part of Russia.

SIBERIANS The inhabitants of Siberia are another type of Russian. Settlers originally came to Siberia in the 17th century to escape the religious reformation under Peter I. They were adherents of the "old faith" and did not recognize the church reforms and modernization; nor would they accept outsiders into their community. They settled in isolation, and have managed, to some extent, to maintain to this day the customs, habits, and dress style of traditional Russia.

In the 19th century, many more people from Ukraine, Belarus, and western Russia migrated to Siberia to escape poverty and in the hope of gaining new land.

Under both the tsars and Communism, Siberia has been used as a place to accommodate political prisoners, and many of Siberia's inhabitants are the descendants of those people.

COSSACKS Cossacks originate from the northern hinterlands of the Black and Caspian Seas. The term was later applied to peasants who fled from serfdom in Poland, Lithuania, and Muscovy to the Dnieper and Don regions, where they established free, self-governing, military communities. Under the Russian umbrella, the Cossacks expanded eastward and were the early colonizers of Siberia.

A Buryat family. The Buryats mainly live in the mountainous area around Lake Baikal and near the Mongolian border.

TURKS Another significant national group are the Turks. These people live mainly around the lower Volga. They include various ethnic groups, such as the Tatars, Bashkirs, Mordvinians, and Udmurts. They tend to have round faces, slanting cheekbones, narrow eyes, and a short and stocky figure inherited from their ancestors who were nomadic horsemen.

MOUNTAIN PEOPLES In the Russian Caucasus there live a variety of peoples and nationalities. These are the peoples of Dagestan (consisting of dozens of small groups and tribes), the Chechens, Ossetians, Karachayevans, Circassians, Cabardins, and Balkars. Each group has its own individual history and customs. The Ossetians, for example, are the last people to speak the language of the ancient Scythians.

PEOPLES OF THE POLAR NORTH In the ice-bound northern extremities of Russia, there live small groups of people generally known as Eskimos. Among them are the Nenets, Chukchis, Komis, Evenks, Yakuts, and Koryaks. These peoples still maintain their ancient languages, which has made them of great interest to philologists and anthropologists.

Some equally small ethnic groups live in the warm south of Asian Russia and in the Far East—the Buryats, Nakasses, Altays, Tuwins, Nganasanes, Yukaghirs, and Tofalars.

POPULATION OF THE RUSSIAN FEDERATION

Russians—119,866,000.
Tatars—5,522,000.
Ukrainians—4,363,000.
Chuvashes—1,774,000.
Bashkirs—1,345,000.
Belorussians—1,206,000.
Mordvinians—1,073,000.
Chechens—899,000.
Germans—842,000.
Udmurts—715,000.
Maris—644,000.
Kazakhs—636,000.
Avars—544,000.

Jews—537,000.
Armenians—532,000.
Buryats—417,000.
Ossetians—402,000.
Yakuts—380,000.
Komis—336,000.
Peoples of the north &
Far East (Nentsis, Evenks,
Chukchi, Yukaghirs,
Nganasanes, Khanty,
Mansi, etc.)—182,000.
Gypsies—153,000.
Poles—95,000.

Greeks—92,000.
Turks—9,900.
Assyrians—9,600.
Chinese—5,200.
Arabs—2,700.
Persians—2,600.
Japanese—600.
Indians & Pakistanis—500.
French—400.
Beluchis—300.
English—200.
Americans—200.

Total (1989)—147,022,000

This census, taken in 1989, is the latest. However, some statistical studies were carried out in October 1993 by the *Delovoy Mir* (*Business World*) newspaper concerning the demographic situation in Russia. The results are given below as a supplement to the above information.

In 1992, for the first time in the postwar period, the population in Russia decreased by 437,000 people (0.03%) over the year. The population decrease was primarily caused by natural population decrease as seen below.

Natural Population Growth in Russia:

	1991	1992	1993 (forecast)
Births	17,946,000	15,876,000	15,740,000
Deaths	16,907,000	18,074,000	18,540,000
Natural growth	1,039,000	–2,198,000	–2,800,000

Under the forecast, migration from the former Soviet republics in 1993 increased Russia's population by another 300,000 people. In the same year, 110,000 people emigrated.

Russia's population in millions (estimates):

1992	1993	1994 (forecast)
148.7	148.7	148.6

LIFESTYLE

THE LIFESTYLE of the urban and village populations in Russia differ sharply, as in most other countries in the world. Russia's cities as a rule are cosmopolitan, with only a few traditional features surviving. Cities in Russia have the same characteristics as cities in Australia, Germany, and the United States, but skyscrapers are lower and the municipal transportion is less developed.

CITY LIFE

The clothes worn by urban folk are of an international style—men usually wear European-style jackets, trousers, shirts, and ties, and women wear dresses or blouses with skirts or slacks. Food has also been internationalized—people living in Moscow can eat Chinese, Korean, Indian, French, Italian, and other cuisines.

The work schedule dominates people's daily routine in the cities. On work days, household chores are done when time permits, and most are done over the weekend. The norm in Russia is a five-day work week with two days off, usually Saturday and Sunday. One of the days off is devoted to household affairs and the other is usually spent on entertainment, walks in a local park, or visits to the cinema, theater, museum, parents, or friends. City dwellers pay little attention to the changing seasons, except perhaps changing their clothes for warmer winter attire when it gets colder. In towns, national and religious differences are less noticeable, and everyone spends their work time and holidays side by side, in the same offices and visiting the same restaurants, theaters, and sports stadiums.

Opposite: **Women dressed in traditional folk costumes typical of the Volga region.**

Above: **Three students outside Moscow University.**

63

Russians of all ages crowd the beaches of the Black Sea coast in the summer months to enjoy the sun before the long, cold winter arrives.

An explosion in the varieties of social activities available in the cities followed the recent political liberalization in Russia. New societies, clubs, and associations have sprung up everywhere, whether political, cultural, artistic, or environmental. People are anxious to take part in free debate and want to be innovative in a society where free expression was suffocated for so many decades. In place of the former Communist Party publications there have appeared new and independent newspapers and magazines, such as *Daily Kommersant* and *Delovaya Gazeta*. Unfortunately the growing prices of newsprint and printing charges have forced some of these publications to close down.

SUMMER ACTIVITIES People from the city usually try to go on vacation in the summer to enjoy the warmth of the northern sun and admire Russia's plethora of flowers, green forests, and meadows. It is an interesting paradox that until recently thousands of people, especially the young, have been deserting their native villages for the cities and, so to speak, for civilization; at the same time millions of city dwellers have been doing the opposite—trying to get closer to the land by joining gardening societies and *dacha* (country chalet) cooperatives. About 20 million urban families spend every weekend from April to October tending their plot of ground—planting vegetables, fruits, flowers, and berries.

THE ARCTIC NORTH

Children who live in the cold northern regions have their own specific amusements and games. They do not fear the long winter, for this is the time to ski, skate, ride dog-pulled sledges, fish through holes cut into the thick ice, and race reindeer.

And what fun it is for children, after spending some time skiing in the freezing cold, to come home and sit by the fire, enjoying thin slices of freshly frozen pink fish meat and drinking sweet, strong tea.

In the summer, Russian city folk particularly enjoy hiking in the forests and meadows and picking berries, nuts, and mushrooms. The children go swimming in the rivers and spend hours tanning themselves in the sun, trying to absorb as much sunlight as they can to last them through the next long winter.

Three workmen enjoy a simple lunch of bread, meat, tomatoes, and wine in a small town in the Omsk region.

COUNTRY LIFE

Life is quite different in the countryside. Even nowadays, when many urban customs have been introduced into village life and many past traditions forgotten, some of the centuries-old customs and rites survive and flourish.

Russia's traditional lifestyle is of a rural nature, since for many centuries most Russians were peasants who worked the land. Village life still depends on the cycle of the seasons; peasants divide the year's work as follows: sowing and harvesting, grazing the cattle, plowing, hay-making, hunting, collecting fruits, stocking up firewood, and spinning.

The annual folk calendar, a crystallization of the wisdom of many generations of country folk, previously regulated their entire life, from birth to death. These traditions have helped the people to survive despite natural disasters and life under both tsarist and Communist repression, and have given their lives a fixed structure.

NATIONAL COSTUMES

Russian national costumes are a real cultural marvel, for they combine both beauty and utility.

For example, in the north, the Eskimos wear fur clothes where every aspect of dress is thoroughly considered to the smallest detail, and where every lace and string has its role to play in making it easier to put the clothes on, button and unbutton them, so nothing should become unfastened at an improper time. With the temperature minus 100°F, a blunder could cost the Eskimos their lives. By contrast, there are the beautiful and intricate decorations that adorn the collar, cuffs, and hems of shirts worn by Russian peasants. These beautiful garments originally fulfilled a superstitious function. The ornaments were called *oberegi* ("ob-er-EG-ih"—the Russian word *oberegat* means "safeguard"), and the embroidery on the men's shirts was meant to safeguard their wearer against evil spirits.

Folk costumes encapsulate the living history of a nation, and for an expert they are an encyclopedia of folk life; they tell a lot about the history of the nation, its mentality, the climate of the country, and many other things. The diversity of Russian costumes is truly fantastic. The Russians alone have hundreds of costumes, with each *gubernia* ("goo-BERN-eeah"—locality)—and sometimes even village—following its own style and fashion. The Buryats have their own costumes, as do the Caucasians and Turks.

CUSTOMS AND FOLKWAYS BASED ON CHRISTIANITY Christianity, which replaced paganism in Russia, added a Christian gloss to the ancient customs, thus making the new religion more understandable to ordinary people. The old Slavic gods were replaced by the Christian saints. The features of Mother-Earth were attributed to the Mother of God; Perun, the god of thunder, became Ilya the Prophet; Veles, the god of cattle, was turned into St. Vlasy, patron saint of domestic cattle; and so on.

An elderly man takes his grandchild out to play in a country park.

Churches were built in the places where the sacred groves and pagan temples used to stand, and people's holidays and rites were, in various ways, adapted to Christian feasts. Gradually, the people adopted the new customs, and church feasts became the most important celebrations of the year, as well as marking significant changes in the yearly cycle.

Thus, since olden times, the winter months of December, January, and February have been a time when people rested after the hard work done in the fall. That is why weddings, Shrovetide fortune telling, and games in the snow were traditionally held at Christmas, Epiphany, and other winter religious festivals.

The farmer, for example, knew that on Candlemas Day (celebrated on February 2) daylight hours would begin to increase, and that on Semoyn's Day, February 3, he was to repair the summer harness for the horses. He also knew that April 8 was the day on which the ice on the river would begin to crack, and on the day of "Alexei, man of God," April 17, the last snows would melt in the fields. On Yegory Veshny's Day, he would drive his cattle to graze and plow his fields.

In this way, the whole year was regulated day by day, and the peasants knew exactly when to pick apples, when to mow oats, and when to celebrate weddings. The life of the peasants was regulated very strictly by the recurring cycle of the four seasons. This tends to make peasants the world over conservative people who are reluctant to change anything in their lives that has been established through the course of centuries.

CUSTOMS AND FOLKWAYS BASED ON OTHER RELIGIONS The natural cycle has the same role in the lives of the other religious groups living in Russia. The Muslims shape their lives according to the precepts of the Koran, observing holidays and feasts, elaborated and adapted by their forefathers. The Buddhists live according to their own rules, as passed on by Gautama Buddha. Although outwardly the customs observed by the Caucasian mountain peoples, the Buddhists from the Kalmyk steppes, the Siberians living in the *taiga*, or the Chukchis who see nothing but ice and snow all the year round differ, all of them customarily follow the same patterns of life dictated by nature and the seasonal changes.

In the northern wastes of Siberia, it is essential that Yakut children wrap up in thick fur clothing to protect them against harsh winter conditions.

EDUCATION

In Russia, education is compulsory and provided by the state, and it begins at the preschool level, when children are five years old. The children play games and are taught to read, write, and count.

Secondary education begins at age six, and lasts for 11 years. Children have to attend school six days a week, Monday to Saturday. The school year begins in September and ends in May. It is divided into four terms, with vacations of up to two weeks between the terms.

Russia also has a number of special vocational high schools, where a general education is mixed with technical training and some on-the-job experience. In a similar style are the junior colleges—places where the students can concentrate on medical, musical, or artistic study, as well as receive a general education. Higher education begins at around age 18 and lasts for five or six years. Again, all higher education is state funded, though students have to attain the appropriate grades to be allowed to continue. Traditionally, Russian higher education has been academically oriented, but it is currently undergoing changes as the system is gearing itself more toward the requirements of industry and commerce.

It has been said that during the period 1965–1985, serious harm was inflicted on the Russian education system and that young people were prevented from demonstrating the true extent of their abilities by perfunctory instruction and the drive for uniformity.

Current reforms being applied in the system are aimed at making it a more democratic institution, where students play a more active role in their own education and do not study just for the sake of obtaining good grades.

Students using computers in Moscow's Air Training School. Nowadays, it is possible to attend private, fee-paying schools in Russia. There is greater competition for college and university places, and so those who get the appropriate grades and are willing to pay fees have an advantage over those who cannot afford the fees.

BIRTH, MARRIAGE, AND DEATH

Traditional rituals connected with birth, coming of age, marriage, and death, are still of an essentially religious nature, despite 70 years of Communism. These rituals, although they differ greatly from religion to religion, actually are observed for the same reasons. Christians baptize their newborns, while Muslims and Jews circumcise their male infants; these two rites have the same symbolic significance of safeguarding the newborn against all evils and calamities and blessing the child with a happy life. Death rites are also similar—relatives and friends pay their respects to the deceased and wish for eternal peace.

Funeral rites being performed at a burial in Smolensk.

Under the Communist system, it was usual to have a local Soviet councillor officiate at weddings, fulfilling the role of priest. Rings and vows were still exchanged. But with Russia's recent liberalization, more people are opting for a traditional-style wedding conducted by a clergyman of their chosen religion. However, divorce has become a serious problem in Russia. In 1991, the divorce rate in the USSR was 40%, and shows no sign of declining.

In the 1920s and 1930s, attempts were made to do away with the old rites and rituals, replacing them with new, "socialist" practices. Easter, Christmas and New Year festivities were abolished and branded as "remnants of the past." Religious feasts were replaced by celebrations of the birthdays of revolutionary leaders and anniversaries of revolutions in various countries. But these new celebrations are not well established and are perceived as artificial by the people. At present, the old festivals are gradually being restored.

RELIGION

TWO MAJOR WORLD RELIGIONS, Christianity (Orthodox) and Islam, have the greatest number of followers in Russia. Small Jewish and Armenian populations and their religions can also be found within the borders of the Russian Federation, as well as Buddhist communities on Russia's southern and eastern borders. Following the Communist authorities' persecution of all religions in Russia for most of this century, many of the churches are currently undergoing a revival in Russia's more liberal climate.

CHRISTIANITY

THE RUSSIAN ORTHODOX CHURCH Christianity, as was noted in previous chapters, came to Russia in the 10th century from Byzantium. Following the East-West schism of 1054, when Christianity was divided into the Orthodox and the Catholic denominations, Christianity's Eastern branch, the Greek Orthodox Church, prevailed in Russia. The translation of the Greek term "orthodox" means "doctrines that are held as right or true," and hence the official name of the Church in Russia is the Russian Orthodox Church. In the course of five or six centuries, Christianity was introduced into pagan Russia with difficulty and often by force, but on the whole, the process happened peacefully, without any massacres of people or mass destruction of towns.

. Later, the Orthodox Church was so firmly established in the lives of the people that it became an integral part of most Russians' consciousness. After the fall of Constantinople to the Ottoman Empire in the middle of the 15th century, Russia became the chief custodian of the precepts of

Opposite: **Cathedral of the Assumption in Cathedral Square, the Kremlin. The cathedral was built in 1479 and is the oldest structure in Cathedral Square. It is also the place where the Russian tsars were crowned.**

Above: **Church banners being carried in a Russian Orthodox procession in St. Petersburg.**

Russian Orthodox clergymen still wear the traditional long, shovel-shaped beard banned by Tsar Peter I.

Orthodoxy and remains so to this day, despite the Communists' attempt to suppress it.

To explain the precepts of Orthodoxy in full is too great a task for this book. We shall only mention that the code of its basic dogmas, the so-called "Creed," binds every follower of the Orthodox religion to believe in the "triune God": in God the Father, who created the earth; God the Son (Jesus Christ), who came from heaven to be born of the Virgin Mary, be crucified under Pontius Pilate, and on the third day be resurrected from the dead and ascend into heaven; and God the Holy Spirit, who proceeded from God the Father. This is set forth in clauses one to eight of the Creed. Clause nine binds the believer to revere the one holy and apostolic church. Clauses 11 and 12 tell the faithful to expect resurrection from death and eternal life after Judgment Day.

The Russian Orthodox Church is headed by the Patriarch of All Russia (currently Alexei II) and does not recognize the Pope.

Some nationalities living in the northern Caucasus, including the northernmost people of northern Ossetia, profess the Orthodox faith, where it originated from Georgia. But many people in this region are Muslims. In the Middle Ages, Christian missionaries preached the new religion among the pagans of northern Russia and Siberia and managed to baptize such groups as the Komis, Permyaks, Maris, and Mordvinians.

In 1990, 18,666 Orthodox communities were officially recorded in the Soviet Union as a whole, most of which were in Russia.

OTHER CHRISTIAN CHURCHES   The Orthodox faith differs from Catholicism in a number of religious beliefs and details pertaining to rites and rituals. Nevertheless, it is more similar to Catholicism than to Protestantism. In the Russian Federation, Catholicism has a small number of followers, chiefly among Poles and Lithuanians who have settled there.

The number of Protestant churches is tiny. There are also various small groups of Evangelists, Seventh-Day Adventists, and Jehovah's Witnesses, whose popularity is growing.

Armenians have been settling in Russia for many centuries. Large Armenian colonies exist in Moscow, St. Petersburg, Rostov-on-Don, Astrakhan, and other large cities. In each of these places, a branch of the Armenian Church was set up. Today, functioning Armenian churches have remained in only a few Russian towns. The Armenian Church is also Christian and is a branch of the so-called Gregorian Church, which, although similar, has some deviations in dogma from both Orthodoxy and Catholicism.

An Orthodox Jewish man prays in a Moscow synagogue.

JUDAISM

Despite a Jewish population of more than 537,000 people, only a small percentage regularly attend the synagogue. This is mainly because Jewish practice was suppressed by the Soviet regime, offering little opportunity for generations of Jews to learn the faith.

Top: **Women pray in a Moscow mosque.**

Bottom: **Buryat Buddhists pray and make offerings at a shrine.**

ISLAM

The Islamic religion has the second largest number of adherents in Russia. It is professed mainly by peoples living in the Volga region—the Tatars and the Bashkirs—and by some peoples of the Northern Caucasus—Chechens, Ingushes, and Dagestanis. They all belong to the Sunni branch of Islam. There are no local variations of the Islamic teachings, and dogmas, customs, and prayers follow exactly those laid down by the Prophet Mohammed.

BUDDHISM

Buddhism, in the form of Lamaism, is the third major world religion to have followers in Russia. Its adherents live in three small republics—Buryat (near Lake Baikal), Kalmyk (on the Caspian Sea), and Tuva (on the Mongolian border).

The Russian tsars favored the Buddhists, although it is not known exactly why. For example, Empress Elizabeth (the daughter of Peter I) proclaimed freedom to profess Lamaism in Russia in 1740, the 250th anniversary of which was widely celebrated amongst the Buddhists of Russia in 1990.

RELIGIOUS PERSECUTION

Ever since the reforms of Peter I, the Russian Orthodox Church has been dependent upon the state. The clergy received salaries from the state and were considered mere state officials "concerned with religious affairs."

Soon after the 1917 Revolution, by a decree of the Soviet powers, the Church was separated from the state and became independent. Its first act was the restoration of the Orthodox Patriarchship, which had been banned by Tsar Peter. Freedom to profess and practice any religion was allowed, and religious belief was henceforth considered a matter of individual conscience. This progressive step made by the Soviet powers put all religions in Russia on an equal footing.

Regrettably, the new authorities did not maintain their even-handed attitude. Atheism became state policy in the 1920s, and this set off a campaign of persecution of the churches and believers. Clergymen of all religions were herded into concentration camps and prisons and were branded as "working people's parasites." Churches and temples were closed down, and their decorations—including those that were of a great artistic and cultural value—were either stolen or destroyed. The buildings were at worst blown up and at best used as storehouses, workshops, or club houses. It is impossible to say now how many churches, mosques, and synagogues were destroyed during this period. Religious literature was confiscated and destroyed, and reading the Bible was equated with counter-revolutionary activity. People were not allowed to baptize their newborns or to perform funeral rites for their dead.

This state of affairs lasted until 1942–1943 when, amidst the heavy casualties of World War II, the state decided to use religion to boost military-patriotic sentiments. Some churches were opened, and people talked about the need to wage a "sacred war" against the non-Orthodox German aggressor. Strange as it might seem, after the war persecution against the church was resumed, first under Stalin and then under the "liberal" Khrushchev. Again, ancient churches were destroyed, icons burned, and believers persecuted. Many churches were turned into museums.

In the 1970s and 1980s, under the pressure of world opinion, the Orthodox Church was allowed to exist, but only if it limit its role to "promoting peace on earth through prayer." In the 1990s, religion was revived in Russia, and the number of followers of different faiths continues to grow. The once confiscated churches, monasteries, and church property have been handed back to the clergy. It has again become a national custom to celebrate religious holidays like Christmas and Easter for Christians, Id-al-Fitr and Id-al-Adha for Muslims, Yom-Kippur for Jews, and Vesak Day for Buddhists, as well as many other festivals.

LANGUAGE

RUSSIANS ACCOUNT FOR FOUR-FIFTHS of the Russian Federation's population, so it is natural that Russian is the most widely spoken language. Although all ethnic groups living in Russia use their own national languages, a knowledge of Russian is something they all have—it is the common language of Russia and the CIS. For example, a Ukrainian would speak Russian to a Buryat.

Before 1991, Russian was the prefered language for all the nations of the republics of the USSR. Russian is also one of the official languages of the United Nations. The Russian language performs all these complicated duties with honor, for it has one of the richest vocabularies and is one of the most flexible and developed languages in the world.

Above: **A letter to the United States. The right-hand side of the letter is written in the Cyrillic script. Note that the country, rather than the person's name, is written first.**

Opposite: **A Communist hardliner protests during the political chaos of 1993. Behind him in Moscow's Pushkin Square is a statue of Alexander Pushkin, a great innovator of Russian language and literature. The hardliner's banner says: "Yeltsin, Gaidar, Luzhkov and company should be held responsible for the disintegration of the country and the humiliation of the people in front of the world."**

HISTORY OF THE RUSSIAN LANGUAGE

Russian belongs to the eastern branch of the Slavic linguistic family. In about the first century B.C., the Slavic languages became isolated from the other Indo-European languages. In the sixth and seventh centuries, the Slavic languages diversified and the Eastern Slavic or old Russian language became one of three branches of the Slavic language. Today, languages of the southern branch are spoken in former Yugoslavia, Macedonia, and Bulgaria, with the western branch spoken in Hungary, Poland, Slovakia, and the Czech Republic.

From the ninth to 12th centuries, Russian was spoken in Kievan Rus, and later (in the 14th to 16th centuries) it became the official language not only in the Moscow state, but also in the Lithuanian and Moldavian princedoms. But the feudal division and two centuries of Tatar-Mongol domination resulted not only in the disintegration of the state, but also of the language.

Reading the newspaper. Currently, Russia's main national newspapers are *Izvestia* ("News"), *Arguments and Facts* (a weekly newspaper), and *Daily Kommersant* (a recent business paper). *Arguments and Facts* entered the Guinness Book of World Records for achieving the highest ever world circulation for a newspaper—26 million copies—in 1991. The old Communist Party broadsheet, *Pravda* ("Truth"), is no longer very popular and represents those who oppose reform.

From the 14th to 16th centuries, three fraternal languages developed—Ukrainian, Belorussian, and Great Russian (or simply Russian). During the same epoch the Moscow dialect began to play a leading role among the numerous other idioms and dialects spoken at that time. It became the basis of a national written language. During Tsar Peter's epoch, the Russian language borrowed many words from western Europe. In particular they made use of scientific, technical, navigational, and administrative terms.

In the 18th and 19th centuries, the language actively developed amidst fighting between the supporters of the older language and the rising new style that brought the literary language closer to the language spoken in the street. A major influence in this debate was Mikhail Lomonosov (1711–1765), who wrote the first scientific grammar of the Russian language, in which words were classified according to "styles"—high, medium, and low.

Major reforms to the language were carried out at the beginning of the 19th century by Alexander Pushkin (1799–1837), the father of Russian literature. Pushkin synthesized a variety of genres—folk, Old Church Slavic, and various western European languages—to create a unified system cemented together by the Moscow dialect of the Russian language. Pushkin is the founder of modern Russian literary language and its phonetic, grammatical, and lexical standards. He has had as much (if not more) influence on the development of the Russian language as Shakespeare has had on English.

Although in the past two centuries the language has changed a lot and the number of words has increased, Russians still mainly speak the language that resulted from Pushkin's reforms.

THE CYRILLIC ALPHABET

The oldest treasures of written Russian date back to the 11th century. Earlier examples have not been preserved, or are as yet undiscovered. Experts believe that some kind of written language existed before this time. For example, a 10th century Arabian traveler mentions that he saw on the tomb of a Russian nobleman some inscriptions and a name. However, it is unknown what kind of inscription this was.

The alphabet of all the Slavic languages that is used today, with some minor differences, by Russians, Ukrainians, Belorussians, Serbs, and Bulgarians, was created in the middle of the ninth century by the brothers Cyril and Methodius. They were two monks involved in translating Byzantine church texts (written in Greek) into the Slavic script. This alphabet consisted of 30 letters—some borrowed from the Greek alphabet and others specifically invented to convey the sounds of the Slavic

Alexander Pushkin is considered the creator of a fully developed Russian literary language. To the later classical writers of the 19th century, Pushkin stands as the cornerstone of Russian literature, and is in novelist Maxím Gorky's words, "the beginning of beginnings."

CYRILLIC	TRANSLIT-ERATION	PRONUNCIATION	CYRILLIC	TRANSLIT-ERATION	PRONUNCIATION
А	a	Father	Р	r	ravioli (rolled r)
Б	b	bit	С	s	Soviet
В	v	vote	Т	t	ten
Г	g	goat	У	u	pool
Д	d	dog	Ф	f	fit
Е	ye	yes	Х	kh	Bach
Ё	yo	yoke	Ц	ts	cats
Ж	zh	azure	Ч	ch	cheer
З	z	zero	Ш	sh	shop
И	i	feet	Щ	shch	fresh sheets
Й	y	boy	Ъ	hardens following vowel	
К	k	kit	Ы	y	shrill
Л	l	let	Ь	softens preceding consonant	
М	m	map	Э	e	bed
Н	n	not	Ю	yu	cute
О	o	owe	Я	ya	yacht
П	p	pat			

The Cyrillic alphabet.

languages that did not exist in Greek. Cyril and Methodius were canonized for their great achievement. When Kievan Rus adopted Christianity in the 10th century, it gained not only books from Byzantium written in Greek, but also books from Bulgaria written in the Slavic script—the Cyrillic alphabet of Cyril and Methodius. This alphabet became the basis of the written Russian language. The Cyrillic alphabet was preserved through the course of centuries in both manuscript form and in the first printed books.

Under Tsar Peter I, the so-called civilian script, which was simpler and more convenient for printing, was introduced. This is the script used today.

The Cyrillic alphabet has also been used to create written languages for those peoples of the USSR that before the 1917 Revolution did not have a written language: the nations of the far north, the Bashkirs, the Buryats, the Kabardino-Balkars, the peoples of Dagestan, the Komis, the Maris, the Mordvinians, and the Yakuts of northern Siberia.

NON-SLAVIC LANGUAGES

Apart from Russian, people in Russia also speak languages belonging to other groups, such as Turkic, Finno-Ugric, and Iranian. There is much about the history of these languages that is not understood.

It has been discovered that the languages of the peoples living in the Urals and the Volga region—the Bashkirs, Udmurts, and Maris—speak languages that are very closely related to Hungarian and Finnic. Scientists believe that these peoples were once related nations who migrated together with the Hunnic hordes of the conqueror Atilla during the great movement of nations in the fourth and fifth centuries. They traveled through the expanses of Asia to Europe and partially settled down, until reaching the Danube River and Pannonia, where they created the Magyar state, now modern Hungary. Some also traveled north and settled in Finland.

Two Russians study movie listings in Moscow. Approximately 150 feature films and 1,000 documentaries are produced in Russian each year. Following Russia's recent political liberalization, movies from all over the world can be seen in Russian cinemas.

A well-known Chukchi author, Yuri Rytkheu, looks through some children's textbooks and fiction on the Chukchi Peninsula, Russia's easternmost point. These books have been published in the indigenous language of the region.

NAMES

Russian names dating back to pagan times have practically died out. Only a few have remained and today sound more like nicknames. Some of them sound almost incomprehensible to modern Russians, for example, Yermak, Zhdan, Kruchina, Metla, Pervoi, Tomilo, Nezhdana, and Shchap.

After the conversion of Rus to Christianity, people began to be given new, Christian names. During the first centuries after conversion the people had two names—an old pagan one, and a new Christian name given in baptism.

There used to exist what is known as *Svyatsy*—a church calendar where every day was marked with the names of saints or Biblical personages. A newborn child would usually be given one of the names falling on the day of his/her birth. Usually, these were names borrowed from the Old or New Testament. From these origins, certain names became nationally popular. For example, Ioann (Ivan), Andrei, Pavel, Pyotr, Filipp, Luka, Matfei (Matvey), and Mikhail; plus female names like Maria, Anna, Marfa, Elizaveta, and Tamara.

This list was increased by names taken from the Byzantine Greeks—Feodor, Georgy (Yuri), Konstantin, Nikolai, Vasily, Alexander, Alexei, Lev, Lydia, Irina, Sofya, Taisia, and others, as well as purely Russian names like Boris, Gleb, Svyatoslav, Vladimir, and names borrowed from Scandinavia—Askold, Oleg, and Igor.

Patronymics (a name derived from the given name of the father) are traditional in Russia. If the father's name is Ivan Krylov, then the son's name, for example, will be Pyotr (given) Ivanovich (patronymic) Krylov (family). Likewise, the daughter's name will be, for example, Natalia Ivanovna Krylov. It is usual among friends and aquaintances to address each other by both the given name and the patronymic.

In the post-revolutionary 1920s, it was the fashion to give "revolutionary" names such as Marat, Zhores, Spartak, and Engels. There were also some very strange names reflecting the new social and political realities—Idea, Raketa, Diktatura, Avangard, Elektron, Revolutsia, and Traktor! There even appeared some ugly names that were abbreviations: Voenmor (the Russian abbreviation for the navy), Melor (Marx, Engels, and Lenin, the founders of the revolution), and even Dazdraperma (the first syllables of the communist slogan "Long Live May Day"). After Lenin's death, there appeared many names that were adaptions of his name. For example, Vladlen, Lenina, Vilen, or Ninel. But all these names have long ceased to be anything but a joke.

Today, the most popular names are those that came from Greek and other European languages. Few names are borrowed nowadays. The only exception is the female name Indira, reflecting Indian prime minister Indira Gandhi's popularity in Russia.

The names of the peoples of the far north are quite original. Some are difficult to pronounce and very complicated: Akhakhanavrak, Kutyakhsiuk, Eketamyn, Yarakvagvig, and Ememkut. As is the case with nations who are in the early stages of their development, these names have clear-cut meanings, much like those traditionally used by Native Americans. Some, like Volna and Groza(wave and thunderstorm), reflect natural phenomena, while others are definitions of human qualities and properties ("he who owns many reindeer," or "one who is not afraid of evil spirits").

A schoolteacher and her class. Nowadays, Russian children are more likely to be given names of a Greek or European origin, such as Ivan, Pyotr, Georgy, Lydia, Nina, or Tamara. Diminutive names are often used when addressing young girls and boys. For example, a girl named Tatyana may also be addressed as Tanya, Tanyusha, or Tanyechka.

ARTS

RUSSIAN ART is justifiably considered a great contributor to world culture. In the course of nine centuries, Russia has produced a number of outstanding works of architecture, painting, music, and literature.

EARLY RUSSIAN ART

For many centuries, Russian architectural styles fell into two types: religious architecture, such as churches and monasteries; and civil architecture, including fortresses, palaces, and houses.

RELIGIOUS ARCHITECTURE In Kievan Rus, churches were the first and best stone structures to be built. In 1037, construction began on St. Sofia's in Kiev. This was Russia's first stone cathedral, and was built by architects who had come from Byzantium.

Gradually, a national type of church developed. It was the so-called "four-pillar church," with its vault supported from the inside by four pillars. A church could have a different number of domes: one (symbol of Jesus Christ), three (symbol of the Trinity), or five (symbol of Jesus Christ and four Apostles). Magnificent 11th and 12th century cathedrals have been preserved in Vladimir, Novgorod, and Pskov, as well as in Kiev in Ukraine.

Russian architecture revived after Rus' liberation from the Mongols and the establishment of the centralized Moscow state at the beginning of the 15th century. The Russian sovereigns paid special attention to consolidating and embellishing their capital city, Moscow. The Kremlin—the tsar's residence—was made particularly beautiful. Under Tsar Ivan III, famous architect Aristotle Fioravanti was invited from Italy and built the magnificent five-domed Cathedral of the Assumption in the Kremlin. Century after century, splendid cathedrals and monastery buildings appeared inside the Kremlin fortress to symbolize the might and unity of the Russian state.

Opposite: **Situated in Red Square, central Moscow, the Cathedral of the Intercession (popularly known as St. Basil's) was built in the 16th century by Tsar Ivan IV to celebrate the capture of Kazan in 1552. Legend has it that on completion of the building the tsar had the two architects, Postnik and Barma, blinded, so that they could not surpass the cathedral's beauty by building any other structure!**

The remarkable St. Basil's Cathedral in Moscow's Red Square is unequalled in Russian architecture. It was built by architects Barma and Postnik on Ivan the Terrible's orders to honor the capture of Kazan in 1552. It is a cluster of nine colorful tower-like churches, each crowned with a dome, all of which are connected by internal vaulted passages and surrounded by a circular gallery.

FORTRESSES AND MONASTERIES From the Middle Ages, every town was surrounded by a strong wall to protect it against enemy attacks. Russian architects built mighty fortresses with towers and walls capable of

The 11th century Lavra Monastery in Kiev, Ukraine, was one of the earliest examples of religious architecture in medieval Rus. The word "Lavra" indicates that it is the principal monastery in the area. The monastery was used as a fortress by the Kievan Russians when the Mongols invaded in 1240.

ICONS

The art of icon painting came to Rus from Byzantium and achieved a very high standard. The icons brought from Constantinople were highly revered and considered sacred in Russia. One of them, "Our Lady of Vladimir" (11th or 12th century), which according to legend was supposed to have been painted by the Apostle Luke, has been miraculously preserved in Vladimir.

An icon is not just an ordinary painting. It is a special type of religious image that the artist imbues with divine energy, so that the image becomes, so to speak, an aspect and expression of God. All icon painting methods are meant to give the image an ethereal quality, in order to illustrate a religious idea. Large eyes are a dominating feature in faces depicted on icons, symbolizing the superiority of the spirit over the body. The background is usually golden-colored and painted in abstract, and is also intended to elevate the representatives of God—the saints and martyrs—from everything earthly.

Before starting work on an icon, the artist prepared himself through long prayer and fasting. It was believed that it was not the artist who was painting the icon, but that divine energy inspired and worked through the artist.

Due to western European influence, icon painting became secularized in the 17th century, with icons taking on a more earthly and realistic appearance.

withstanding assaults and long sieges. In the 16th century, the architect Fyodor Kon designed the walls and towers of the White City, which encircled the central part of Moscow, as well as the defensive structures of the fortress town of Smolensk, at that time one of the most powerful in all of Europe. Fortresses can still be found in Tula, Novgorod, Pskov, and Astrakhan.

The monasteries, too, were encircled by powerful walls and towers. They were sometimes used as fortresses so that during enemy invasions shelter could be provided for refugees while withstanding fierce assaults and sieges. Particularly well fortified were Troitse-Sergieva Lavra Monastery in the Moscow vicinity, which withstood a 24-month siege by Polish soldiers, and the Solovetsky and Kirillo-Belozersky monasteries (both in the north). Many of them have been preserved and can still be seen.

A staircase in the baroque Catherine Palace. Situated in the town of Pushkin near St. Petersburg, the Catherine Palace (named after Tsar Peter I's wife) was completed in 1723. Peter's daughter Elizabeth ascended the throne in 1742 and decided to use the place as her summer residence. An extravagant tsarina, she lavished enormous sums of money on the interior decor.

17TH AND 18TH CENTURY DEVELOPMENTS

In all spheres of life, the 17th and 18th centuries were a time of the breakdown of the old and the establishment of the new in Russia. The most noticeable changes occurred in architecture, with the building of the new capital of St. Petersburg in 1703. The architects invited from Holland, Italy, and Germany built a city that was more European than Russian.

Most of the buildings of Tsar Peter's time were rebuilt later in the 18th century, but some have been preserved to this day and give an idea of the epoch: the St. Peter and Paul Cathedral, the palace of Peter I in the Summer Garden, and Menshikov's Palace (all in St. Petersburg).

During Catherine II's reign, a number of highly gifted architects were active, and their buildings still adorn many Russian towns. One of the most prominent architects was Bartolomeo Rastrelli (1700–1771), an Italian who came to Russia as a boy. He became a prominent figure of the Russian national school of architecture. He built many palaces and churches in St.

Petersburg and other towns, and created his own school of architecture. Among his works are the Winter Palace and the palaces of Peterhof and Tsarskoye Selo. By lavishly embellishing the palaces with slender symmetrical columns, statues, and stucco decorations, he created an impression of classical festivity. Rastrelli became the founder of a new architectural style—Russian baroque.

Carlo Rossi (1775–1849), the son of an Italian actress, embellished St. Petersburg with the Mikhailovsky Palace (now the Russian Museum), and added the finishing touches to the Dvortsovaya (Palace) and Senate Squares. In Moscow, he also supervised the building of the Main Headquarters and the beautiful Theatralnaya Street.

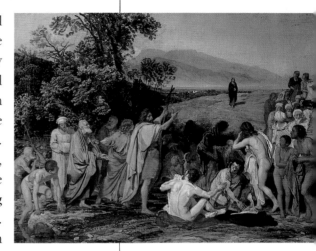

Christ Appears to the People **by Alexander Ivanov. This monumental work took 25 years to complete.**

PAINTING

European-style portrait painting developed in Russia in the 18th century, replacing icon painting, and realistically portrayed actual people. At first, only the upper classes and gentry were depicted—the great lords and the tsars. I. Argunov, who was born a peasant, first painted the life and faces of the common people. His most famous portrait, *A Girl in a Head-Band*, depicts a peasant woman.

A. Venetsianov (1780–1847) devoted his work to peasant life, depicting it in a very idealized manner. Several schools of art developed in the mid-1800s and artists began to paint more varied subjects.

The work of Alexander Ivanov (1806–1858) stands somewhat by itself. In his monumental canvas *Christ Appears to the People*, which took a quarter of a century to complete, he set forth his ideas about life, religion, and the painful expectations and desire for freedom.

Ilya Repin's painting *The Cossacks Drafting a Letter to the Turkish Sultan.*

Realism affirmed itself in the early 1860s through a group of artists led by Ivan Kramskoi. They broke with the officially-backed Moscow Academy and formed a commune of free artists. In 1870, the group became the Association of Mobile Exhibitions. They traveled round the country demonstrating the latest artistic innovations. These artists became known as *peredvizhniki* ("per-ed-VIJ-nee-keh"—means "the wanderers"). The most famous of them was Vasily Perov (1834–1882). His paintings present a panorama of Russian life in that epoch. There was no subject he considered unworthy of his art—poor children pulling a barrel of icy water on a sledge, a common funeral, a rural religious procession with a drunken priest—all aspects of life were depicted on his canvases.

Vasily Vereshchagin (1842–1904), painted many battle scenes, laying bare the essential inhumanity of war. His most famous canvas *The Apotheosis of War* depicts a huge mountain of skulls—the result of one of the campaigns of the ancient conqueror Tamerlane—and bears the following inscription: "To all the conquerors of the past, present and future." The heroes of folk and epic tales can be seen on the canvases of Victor Vasnetsov (1848–1926). The most famous of them, *The Epic Heroes,* depicts the legendary men who defended Russia against the Mongol invasion.

One of the most famous Russian artists of the 20th century is Marc Chagall (1887–1985). Forced to leave Russia due to difficulties with the Communist authorities, he spent much of his time in exile, mainly in France. He was a prolific painter and book illustrator (he illustrated Gogol's *Dead Souls*), and many of his works have religious themes.

ILYA REPIN

The great realist artist Ilya Repin (1844–1930) was closely linked with the ideas of the *peredvizhniki*. Repin excelled in all genres and was an innovator in each. In the 1870s, his best canvas was *The Volga Haulers* (below). He devoted a whole series of canvases to the revolutionary movement— *The Arrest of a Political Offender*, *Refusal to Confess*, and *Unexpected Homecoming*. Among Repin's most popular historical paintings were *The Cossacks Drafting a Letter to the Turkish Sultan* and *Ivan the Terrible and His Son Ivan*, the latter depicting the historical fact of the tsar killing his son in a fit of fury. The summit of Repin's work is the huge ensemble *Meeting of the State Council*, in which the country's highest bureaucracy meeting under the chairmanship of the tsar is presented without romanticism.

19TH CENTURY LITERATURE

The 19th century has been called the "golden age" of Russian art and culture, for it was then that Russia's greatest works were created in literature, painting, and music.

Alexander Pushkin (1799–1837), Russia's most prominent national poet, is considered the father of modern Russian literature. His many works—*Yevgeny Onegin* (1823–1831), a verse novel, *The Tales of Belkin* (1830), a cycle of realistic stories (the first in Russia), the historical drama *Boris Godunov* (1825), and hundreds of poems—are considered the treasure of Russian literature. He was on friendly terms with the Decembrists, the first Russian revolutionaries, whom he did not denounce even after their defeat. In an effort to subdue and win over the famous poet, Tsar

Nicholas I appointed him to court service, which eventually led to his early death. Tormented by the nobility and persecuted by creditors, he died defending his honor in a duel with a Frenchman. Crowds of people came to his apartment in St. Petersburg to pay their last respects. Pushkin's work represents in embryonic form almost all the literary genres that developed later in the 19th century.

Mikhail Lermontov (1814–1841), whose reputation as a lyricist is second only to Pushkin's, became famous after writing his elegy "On the Death of the Poet." It was devoted to Pushkin, for whose death he blamed high society. In his famous novel, *A Hero of Our Time* (1840), he describes the typically redundant and idle nobleman of Nicholas' Russia.

The work of Nikolai Gogol (1809–1852) marks an important stage in the development of Russian literature. In his poetic novel *Dead Souls* (1842–1852), and play *The Inspector-General* (1836), he illustrated in satirical form the vices specific not only to Russia with its serfdom, but to all of mankind—the ignorance, legalized corruption, greed, and self-interest of the bureaucracies that accompany absolutist governments and societies. Gogol was the first to portray in literature the "little" man—the world of urban commoners, petty officials, paupers, and the destitute. Gogol's story, *The Overcoat* (1842), is considered a classic of the Fantastic genre, and marks the beginning of a new democratic trend in Russian literature.

REALISM In the middle of the 19th century, a more realistic style of literature came into prominence. This literature was characterized by its rich and detailed imagery, profound psychological description, and social realism.

Ivan Turgenev (1818–1883) is highly representative of this style. In *A Sportsman's Sketches* (1852), he realistically portrays life in the Russian countryside. This book was considered to have played an important part in preparing public opinion for the abolition of serfdom. Turgenev was a keen observer of public life and reflected rising political and social questions in his famous novels *Rudin* (1856), *On the Eve* (1860), and *Fathers and Sons* (1862).

The work of Fyodor Dostoyevsky (1821–1881) still continues to have an enormous influence on world literature. Unequalled in his gift for psychological penetration, he understood better than anyone the torment of the "little man," the humiliated, insulted, and oppressed people of tsarist Russia. His novels *Crime and Punishment* (1865–1866), *The Brothers Karamazov* (1879–1880), and *The House of the Dead* (1861–1862) are among the great works of world literature.

The second half of the 19th century saw the rise of writer Leo Tolstoy (1828–1910). In his novels *War and Peace* (1865–1869), *Anna Karenina* (1875–1877), and *Resurrection* (1899), he vividly reflected post-reform life in Russia, with all its complexities and contradictions.

The short-story writer and playwright Anton Chekhov (1860–1904) often wrote about the boredom and frustration of life. Three of his well-

A 1908 photograph of Leo Tolstoy. His autobiographical *A Confession* (1882) gives an account of the spiritual crisis that marked a new direction in his writing.

THE SILVER AGE

The brief period from the beginning of the 20th century to World War I is often called the "Silver Age" of Russian art, for it rounded off the brilliant culture of the preceding century and witnessed the beginning of its disintegration.

In the literary field, Maxim Gorky's (1868–1936, pictured) remarkable romantic stories about tramps, gypsies, and robbers—people who rejected bourgeois values—were coming into vogue.

During the reaction and disillusionment after the 1905 Revolution, Fedor Sologub's novels, with their "cult of death," mysticism, and "satanism," and Leonid Andreyev's gloomy, mystical stories both became highly fashionable.

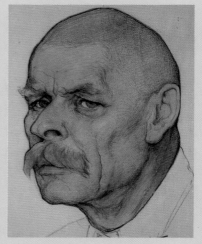

However, it was poetry that gained greatest prominence. A brilliant galaxy of poets appeared of various and often mutually hostile trends—the symbolists Valery Bryusov and Andrei Bely and the futurists Vladimir Mayakovsky and David Burlyuk were the best known. Alexander Blok (1880–1921) was the most prominent poet of the epoch, and wrote highly subjective and mystically tinged poetry. His lyrical verse, in which he speculated about the destiny of the country, was widely read in Russia.

known plays are: *Uncle Vanya* (1900), *The Three Sisters* (1901), and *The Cherry Orchard* (1904). His developments in the short story genre influenced many other writers in Europe.

MUSIC AND BALLET

MUSIC In the 19th century, Russian musical genius blossomed. Peter Tchaikovsky (1840–1893) is probably Russia's all-time greatest composer. His six symphonies, the operas *Yevgeny Onegin*, *Queen of Spades*, and *Mazepa* (all based on Pushkin's literary works), and the ballets *Swan Lake*, *Nutcracker*, and *Sleeping Beauty*, represent collectively the summit of Russian musical art. The composer could convey, with tremendous force, the joy, suffering, and conflicts of mankind. Tchaikovsky's works are still popular the world over.

The works of other composers—Modest Mussorgsky, Alexander

Borodin, and Nikolai Rimsky-Korsakoff—are also acknowledged masterpieces of 19th century Russian music.

In the 20th century, the traditions of the previous century were continued by the brilliant composers Alexander Skriabin, who reflected the approaching momentous social changes, Sergei Rachmaninoff, who spent much of his life in exile in Europe and the United States, and Igor Stravinsky, composer of the popular *Rites of Spring*.

BALLET Russian ballet is considered perhaps the greatest in the world. There are two main ballet companies in Russia: the Bolshoi in Moscow, and the Kirov in St. Petersburg. Both are world-renowned.

At the beginning of the 20th century, the impresario Sergei Diaghilev (1872–1929) organized extremely successful tours in Europe for his company Ballets Russes,

Russian ballet dancers.

starring probably the greatest dancer the world has ever seen, Vaslav Nijinsky (1890–1950). Nijinsky gained legendary status for his extraordinary dramatic virtuosity, strength, and featherweight lightness of movement.

Russia's greatest female dancer was Anna Pavlova (1881–1931). She also toured with Diaghilev's company, and achieved international fame for her discipline, grace, and poetic style of movement. Rudolf Nureyev (1938–1991) was Russia's best-known postwar dancer; a master of fast turns and suspended leaps, he is considered the true heir of Nijinsky.

Above: **A mosaic on the Moscow subway celebrates Communist brotherhood.**

Opposite, bottom: **A small village on the Volga River, Krasnoye, has long been famous for producing jewelry and silverware of exquisite craftsmanship.**

THE SOVIET PERIOD

The years directly following the 1917 Revolution were a period of relative creative freedom, when many of the pre-revolutionary groups and schools in literature and art continued to function. Writers, poets, and artists tried to understand the changes brought about by the revolution and to take part in the new egalitarian life. The period up until Stalin's rise in 1924 produced quite a number of brilliant literary works: Mayakovsky's poems, satirical stories by Mikhail Bulgakov, plus Ilya Ehrenburg's *The Life and Adventures of Julio Jurenito*, Yuri Olesha's *Three Fat Men*, Alexei Tolstoy's historical and fantastic novels *Aelita, Engineer Garin,* and *His Death Ray*, and Mikhail Sholokhov's *And Quiet Flows the Don.*

In music, the young and gifted Sergei Prokofiev, Dimitri Shostakovich, and Aram Khachaturian were composing their first works. The cinema, a new type of art, was rapidly developing. The films of those years were shown with great success throughout the world: Sergei Eisenstein's *Battleship Potemkin*, Vsevolod Pudovkin's *Mother*, N. Ekk's *Road to Life*, and the Vasilyev brothers' film *Chapayev*.

Under Stalin's oppressive presence, art in the 1930s, 1940s and 1950s became totally politicized and had only one function—to provide propaganda for Communist Party policy, which in fact meant the uncritical glorification of the party and its leader, Stalin. Nothing noteworthy has remained from this period.

Stalin's death in 1953 was followed by a revival of artistic activity during

the brief period of Khrushchev's "thaw." The Soviet films *The Cranes Are Flying* and *The Ballad of a Soldier* won world acclaim. Bulgakov's novel *The Master and Margarita* was published in 1966, having spent a quarter of a century in the archives. Another event was the publication of Alexander Solzhenitsyn's story *One Day in the Life of Ivan Denisovich* (1962), where, for the first time in literature, the subject of Soviet concentration camps was frankly discussed.

This period did not last long. Writer Boris Pasternak was forced in 1957 to publish his novel, *Doctor Zhivago*, in Italy, after constant persecution. Pasternak was awarded the Nobel prize for literature in 1958. At a Moscow art exhibition, Khrushchev himself trampled underfoot some non-conventional art not to his liking. These events put an end to the brief "thaw." From 1965 to 1985, very little art of any genuine worth was produced due to the strict censorship. The boldest and most unique in art was smuggled abroad and published there, including Solzhenitsyn's *The Gulag Archipelago* (1973–1975), which caused him to be deported by the authorities. He was awarded the Nobel prize for literature in 1970.

Censorship continued until 1985, when, during the *perestroika* ("peh-reh-STROI-kah") period proclaimed by Mikhail Gorbachev, freedom of speech gradually reemerged. Books that had lain in writer's desks or archives were now published. These included novels by Evgeny Zamyatin, and poems and verse by Pasternak, Osip Mandelstamm, and Anna Akhmatova.

LEISURE

TYPES OF RECREATION IN RUSSIA do not differ from those accepted in the rest of the world. Russians like to visit their friends and play host to guests. When visiting friends, relatives, or parents, it is customary to bring along simple gifts—for example, a homemade pie, a box of candy, a bottle of wine, and perhaps a toy for the host's children.

PASTIMES

In the summer, Russians like to go swimming in their local river or lake, and go mushroom- and berry-picking in the forests. This is easy for villagers, but not for townspeople, who have to make a trip to the countryside by train or car. Village recreational facilities are now similar to those in the towns. During the Soviet years, recreational centers were built in the villages, containing enough room for a library and movie theater, as well as space for all kinds of other activities, such as singing, dancing, and painting.

Village people can also visit a theater or museum in the nearest town: in Russia, even the smaller towns have their own local museums—often rather good ones—built, as a rule, before the 1917 Revolution by rich patrons of the arts. Often, the rich merchants, after collecting a number of paintings, built a special house for the collection and presented it to their hometown.

The most famous among them was Pavel Tretyakov, a Moscow merchant who owned a large collection of 18th and 19th century Russian art. He presented his art collection to the city of Moscow at the end of the last century. Today, it bears the name of its founder and is one of the biggest museums in the world, called the State Tretyakov Gallery.

Above: **Two boys playing chess, an enormously popular pastime in Russia.**

Opposite: **A group of young Russian men play cards to a backdrop of Communist memorabilia in Moscow's Arbat Street.**

On the whole, the type of recreation Russians choose depend upon their personal inclinations—some prefer to lie on the couch reading a book, others like to play a game of chess (chess is extremely popular in Russia), and still others like to tinker with their car over the weekend.

For the mobile, wealthy, and young there are such active pastimes as country hikes, mountain climbing, and journeys down *taiga* rivers in canoes and kayaks. For people living in the north of Russia, the most favored recreation is traveling to the south and the Black Sea coast to the warm sea, to get as much sun as they can to last them through the long northern winter.

In recent times television has become extremely popular, especially among children. Viewers in the main urban centers have three major television channels to watch—two national, and one local channel for that particular republic. Some regions have a greater number of channels. Moscow, for example, has an additional number of channels for educational purposes, and both Moscow and St. Petersburg can receive each other's local television stations.

Above: **Russia's long, snow-covered winters make skating a popular leisure activity.**

Opposite: **Russia's Olga Mostepanova, gold medalist for beam exercises in the 1983 World Gymnastic Championships and holder of the USSR Cup for 1984.**

Television has also been used as an efficient instrument for testing and analyzing Russia's recent spirit of openness, known as *glasnost* ("GLAHZ-nost"). Many programs have been shown discussing and assessing the recent political and social upheavals in Russia and the rest of the USSR. Some parliamentary sessions have also been televised.

PHYSICAL ACTIVITY, EXERCISE, AND SPORTS

Like many countries in the world, Russia has practiced since ancient times various physical exercises, games, and contests, as both a form of education and to prepare young Russians for times of war and hardship. In the early half of the 19th century, sports schools, clubs, and societies began to appear in Moscow, St. Petersburg, and Kiev. Regular sports competitions were held in the country, financed by rich landowners, merchants, and aristocrats. In the late 19th century, workers' sports organizations also began to appear in Russia.

In 1896, P. Lesgarf instigated a scientifically-based system of physical education called Courses for Physical Training that became the prototype of most sports institutes created in the USSR after the 1917 Revolution. Russia was one of 12 countries in 1894 that decided to revive the Olympic Games and set up the International Olympic Committee.

After the 1917 Revolution, sports and physical training became an integral part of life in the USSR. In the 1930s, fitness programs were instituted to prepare people for work and defense. The benefit of these programs became evident during World War II, when the Russian people were tested to the limits of their endurance by the hardships of war.

Today, sports are both voluntary and compulsory in Russia. Compulsory exercise programs are a part of the school curriculum, from kindergarten to college level, as well as in the army. In many industries, people briefly

Cyclists race through the streets of Moscow.

interrupt their working day to exercise. Voluntary sports are practiced via a wide range of sports clubs, organizations, and groups. This network previously belonged to the trade unions and was wholly financed by them.

Russia's major sports societies—CSKA (the Central Sports Army Club), Spartak (the trade unions), Lokomotiv (railway workers), and Dinamo (the Interior Ministry)—have major soccer, basketball, and ice-hockey teams that are popular with millions of fans in Russia. Baseball is also becoming popular, and the first national baseball championships were held in 1989.

Because of the recent reforms in Russia, many sportsmen and women are now turning professional, a status previously not allowed under the Communist system. Sports stars and members of national teams are now paid regular salaries rather than stipends for their services. They also sign regular contracts. Over the last few years, a number of Russia's top soccer players have moved to Europe to play for teams there, where players' salaries are far more generous than in Russia.

In 1989, almost all the leading basketball players of the gold medal

Soviet team in the 1988 Olympic Games in Seoul signed contracts with the NBA in the United States, as well as with clubs in Spain and Germany.

OLYMPICS In 1980, Moscow was the location of the 22nd Olympic Games. This indicated recognition of the USSR's sporting achievements from the world sporting community. But the games were marred by the lack of participation of some 60 nations, including the United States, in protest against the Soviet Union's invasion of Afghanistan in December 1979. But a total of 5,923 competitors representing 81 nations did eventually take part. During these games, 36 world, 74 Olympic, and 40 European records were set. Soviet sportsmen set 14 world and 32 Olympic records. Russia has been a major sporting power in all Olympic events since World War II. Between 1958 and 1988, the USSR won 64 gold medals in track and field events, and 69 gold medals in gymnastics—a traditionally strong sport for Russian athletes. The USSR won another 310 gold medals over the same period in both the winter and summer Olympics.

Cross-country skiers begin a race near Murmansk in Russia's frozen north.

FESTIVALS

AFTER THE 1917 REVOLUTION, all religious holidays were abolished in the USSR and branded as "vestiges of the past." Together with such Christian holidays as Christmas and Easter, the Muslim Ramadan, and the Jewish Yom Kippur, a ban was also imposed on folk holidays like Shrovetide, New Year, *Sabantui* ("Sah-bant-OOEH") and *Navruz* ("Nahv-ROOZ"). Later, many of these celebrations (for example, Shrovetide) were revived because of their ancient pagan origins. The old holidays were forcibly replaced by new ones that usually celebrated some aspect of the Revolution or the new political dogmas. The people accepted some of these holidays and willingly celebrated them. But recent political changes have affected people's attitude towards these festivals.

Holidays in Russia can be divided into several groups.

POLITICAL AND PATRIOTIC HOLIDAYS

First among political holidays is National Day (November 7), the anniversary of the 1917 Revolution. Today, the significance and value of the Revolution is being reassessed, but the anniversary continues to be marked in Russia, though not celebrated with the vigor of old.

Previously, this event was marked by a number of events—a festive meeting of the party and state leaders in the Bolshoi Theater in Moscow; an anniversary report on the economic situation in the country delivered by a member of the Politburo of the Communist Party Central Committee; a military parade and demonstration in Moscow's Red Square and in the Dvortsovaya Square in Leningrad (now St. Petersburg); as well as demonstrations in all regional capitals. In the evenings, people visited each other and celebrated with a festive meal.

Opposite: **A Christmas tree decorates the center of the massive GUM department store in Moscow.**

Below: **People celebrate National Day (November 7), the anniversary of the 1917 Revolution, in Moscow's Red Square. Red carnations are carried as a symbol of bloody revolution.**

Another holiday, May 1, the Day of International Solidarity of Working People (known as Labor Day in many countries, and originally intended to commemorate the police shooting of workers in Chicago, Illinois, in 1886), was celebrated in much the same manner. Today, the nature of the May Day celebration has changed and it is now called Spring Holiday.

Another public holiday is International Women's Day (March 8), which has a rather interesting history. The celebration was instituted by Clara Zetkin, a veteran German Communist Party leader, as a day of struggle for women's rights. But it gradually lost its political content and became just Women's Day, on which it was customary for men to present women with flowers, pay them compliments, and perhaps do all the domestic chores

Tanks go to Moscow's Red Square every May 9, to take part in the military parade to mark the capture of Berlin in 1945.

around the house (much like Mother's Day in the United States).

Victory Day, Russia's most popular patriotic holiday, is celebrated on May 9—the day hostilities ceased in World War II. Military parades are held in Red Square in Moscow, fireworks are exploded over the city, wreaths are laid at the tombs of those who gave their lives fighting for their country, and the surviving war veterans are feted. On this day, a minute's silence is observed in commemoration of those who died defending their country in two world wars.

TRADITIONAL HOLIDAYS

Russia's most popular holidays are of an ancient and traditional origin, and many of the celebrations date back to pre-Christian times. They have much in common with festivals celebrated in other parts of Europe.

NEW YEAR New Year is celebrated with much vigor in Russia and includes a brightly decorated Christmas tree and the exchanging of New Year gifts followed by a hearty dinner. According to tradition, an abundant meal signifies an abundant New Year.

SHROVETIDE Another popular holiday, Shrovetide (called Butter Week in Russia), occurs the day before Ash Wednesday, the first day of Lent in the Christian calendar. People sit down to a festive meal because it is traditionally the last chance to feast before the fasting period of Lent. The highlight of this holiday is the eating of *bliny* ("BLEE-nee"—pancakes), a symbol of Yarilo, the ancient pagan sun-god. It is also a time to announce the coming of spring, and a straw figure representing winter is burned at a carnival.

Farewell to winter! Butter Week, or Shrovetide, is a celebration of pre-Christian Slavic origin. An effigy of winter is burned to welcome the arrival of spring.

SABUNTUI, SURKHARBAN, AND NAVRUZ

Many of Russia's ethnic groups have their own spring holidays that are connected with the completion of the sowing of spring crops. *Sabantui* is celebrated by the Tatars, and *Navruz* by other Muslim peoples, but the essentials are the same for all—to express joy for the coming summer harvest. The name *Sabantui* is thought to have come from an old nomadic tribe called the Saban. The word later came to mean "plough" and "spring crops." The word *tui* means celebration. Hence the word *Sabantui* has come to mean the festival marking the sowing of spring crops. In the days

HOLIDAY SONGS

The singing of ditties called *chastushkas* was at one time a prominent feature of Russian country festivals and parties. In certain parts of rural Russia they still remain popular. A *chastushka* is a verse of four lines sung in a dance rhythm to the accompaniment of a *balalaika* (a stringed instrument similar to a guitar) or Russian accordion.

The song is usually a humorous improvisation on recent local news, in which two performers compete with each other to the general merriment and encouraging applause of the listeners. Both men and women participate.

In modern times, the *chastushka* has moved from rural parties to the variety stage, though it is not as popular as it used to be since it cannot compete with pop music. Yet pointed and clever ditties can still be heard at many rural gatherings.

leading up to *Sabantui*, farmers make little presents for children, such as painted eggs, sweet cookies, and buns. On the day itself, people compete in games such as running, wrestling, the three-legged race, the sack race, and an egg-and-spoon race. All are fiercely contested and popular, and provide those watching with an amusing and exciting spectacle.

The Buryats have a similar holiday, *Surkharban* ("Soor-kah-BAHN"), that is also celebrated in the summer after the crops have been sown. Archery competitions are the main event, as well as wrestling and horse racing. Among the Muslims of Asian Russia, the most important festival is *Navruz*. It is celebrated particularly by the Uzbeks and Tajiks—the peoples of two former Soviet republics. In the towns and villages, people take to the streets to celebrate the arrival of spring by carrying bouquets of flowers and singing songs to honor the blossoming of nature.

RELIGIOUS HOLIDAYS In the past few years, the once-loved Christian celebrations of Christmas and Easter, and the Muslim holidays of Ramadan and Prophet Mohammed's birthday, have all been revived. They are celebrated much as in any other part of the Christian or Muslim world.

FOOD

RUSSIA IS A MULTI-ETHNIC COUNTRY where, as one would expect, there is a wide variety of national cuisine, with practically every ethnic group having its own style of cooking and favorite dishes. Several main styles of food can be singled out.

RUSSIAN CUISINE

Today, Russian cuisine enjoys great popularity throughout the world, and some dishes have been included on international restaurant menus.

Russian cuisine has had a long history, stretching back almost 15 centuries. Because of this, the dishes eaten today are quite different from those of the Russians' distant forefathers. Nevertheless, it is precisely from Russia's long history that the main national dishes originate: rye bread, *bliny* (pancakes), pies, *kasha* ("KAH-shah"—a kind of gruel), plus other

Opposite: **A father plays the accordion to his son following a typical Russian meal including bread, tomatoes, and vodka. Father and son wear traditional costumes.**

Left: **A woman sells sandwiches and pastries in Moscow's Arbat Street. This is one of Moscow's most popular areas for people to stroll around and is well provided with cosy cafés, and shops selling jewelry, and secondhand books and prints.**

Street vendors cook *shashlyk* ("shash-LIK"), or lamb kebabs, on skewers, providing a nourishing meal in the cold winters. Kebabs are a Caucasian dish from Russia's southwestern region.

dishes made from vegetables, mushrooms, nuts, and berries.

The Christian Church, which specified a Lenten diet, had a strong influence on Russian cuisine. According to the old church calendar, 192 to 216 days per year were Lenten days (a time when people are allowed to eat only vegetables, mushrooms, and fish, but no meat). Add to this the fact that meat, milk, and eggs were previously something the common people could afford only on major holidays, and it is understandable why Russian traditional cuisine abounds in dishes made from grain (for example, *kasha*), vegetables (in particular cabbage, carrots, potatoes, onions, turnips, and peas), berries, mushrooms, and herbs prepared in a variety of ways, especially boiled, salted, or baked.

The non-Lenten diet—roasted meat, game, and poultry—was more characteristic of the ruling classes and the gentry and was borrowed mainly from Europe, in particular France, Poland, and Germany. The difference between the diet of the common people and the ruling classes in Russia

THE INDULGENT TSARS

Here is an interesting excerpt from Alexei Tolstoy's (1817–1875) popular historical novel, *Prince Serebrenni* (1874), in which he offers a fictional account of an extravagant feast given by Tsar Ivan the Terrible in the 16th century:

"A great many servants in velvet coats stood before the Tsar, bowed to him, and soon returned, carrying some 200 fried swans on gold trays. Thus began the dinner .... When they had eaten the swans, the servants returned with some 300 fried peacocks, whose fine tail feathers swayed over every dish. The peacocks were followed by fish, chicken meat and cheese pies, *bliny* of all varieties, plus different patties and fritters. While the guests were eating, the servants carried around scoops and goblets of mead .... Although they had spent more than four hours at the table, they were only half way through the meal. The Tsar's cooks really excelled themselves on that day. The huge fishes caught in the Northern Seas aroused special amazement. The silver and gold basins, which had to be carried by several people, were hardly big enough for the fishes. The hares in noodles were also delicious and the guests missed neither the quails in garlic sauce nor the larks spiced with onions and saffron. But then at a sign from the table-dressers, the salt, pepper and vinegar, as well as the meat and fish dishes were taken off the tables. The servants brought into the chamber an 180 pound sugar Kremlin and put it on the Tsar's table. It was followed by a 100 gilded and painted trees on which instead of fruits were hanging treacle- and honey-cakes, as well as other sweetmeats ..."

Such extravagance, which sounds fantastic today, was possible only at the tsar's table. It illustrates that there is much in the Russian cuisine to satisfy any guest!

was always great until the 20th century. This gap became particularly noticeable in the 15th and 16th centuries, when the aristocrats indulged in extravagant and ostentatious feasts. For example, at feasts given by the tsars, sometimes as many as 200 dishes would be served.

Everyone who sits down for a Russian meal is first served bread. Russian bread is very special—it is a favorite with all the Slavic peoples—and it is prepared not from ordinary wheat, but from rye. It has a dark color, is soft and spongy in texture, and has a remarkably pleasant flavor. In Russia, ordinary wheat bread is also baked, but the rye bread is considered far superior and a real treat for foreigners who have not been initiated into this culinary delight.

People celebrate the New Year with a sumptuous meal and sparklers in this St. Petersburg home. Christmas and the New Year are traditional times for Russians to feast.

THE RUSSIAN MEAL

All Russian tables are laid out to include a plate of bread, salt, pepper, and mustard. A guest is first served cold appetizers—cold meat, ham, smoked fish, and vegetables. This also includes the typical Russian salted and marinated tomatoes and cucumbers, plus mushrooms, apples, and of course, red and black caviar. All these typical Russian appetizers are usually washed down with a glass of vodka.

On most Russian menus there are dozens of soups and broths, but the classical opening dish for any meal is *shchi* ("shee") and fish soup, a combination served for more than a thousand years. *Shchi* is a vegetable soup in which cabbage (fresh or sour), potatoes, onions, garlic, carrots, roots, and spices are compulsory ingredients. *Shchi* has a unique flavor created by the cabbage brine and other ingredients. This flavor is the result of the *shchi* being cooked in an oven. *Shchi* soup is usually served with sour cream or milk. The soup is particularly delicious if eaten with rye bread. The remarkable popularity of this dish is explained by its exquisite taste, which once tried is rarely tired of, even if eaten every day of the year.

Ukha ("OO-kah") is a hot fish soup prepared from three or four types of fish with potatoes, onions, spices, and herbs added. It is particularly tasty when prepared in the open on the bank of a river where the fish, so to speak, jumps into the kettle straight from the water. This kind of soup is called *rybatskaya ukha* ("rye-BAHTS-kaiyah"), fisherman's soup.

Russian main courses are also served hot. This is usually a fish or meat dish, boiled or fried and garnished with vegetables. Most of these dishes do not differ much from those found in central Europe. Purely Russian main courses are *kasha*, *bliny*, and a variety of pies.

Kasha is a thick or semiliquid dish made from different cereals, which along with the *shchi* is another thousand-year-old favorite national dish. *Kasha* can be made of peas and ground or whole grains (buckwheat, wheat of different grades, oats, and rice). *Kasha* may be served liquid (as a thin gruel) or thickened, and either sweetened, salted, or unflavored. The method of preparing is very simple and has been tested through the course of centuries: the ingredients are put into boiling water, cooked, and then well stewed. According to taste, it can be served with sugar, salt, butter, vegetable oil, or gravy.

Bliny is considered the pride of Russian cuisine. This dish has been passed down from the distant pagan past, perhaps from the ninth century, and resembles pancakes. *Bliny* requires a minimum of flour with a maximum of water or milk, since a very thin batter is needed. Russian *bliny* are soft, porous, and fluffy, and like a sponge absorb all the melted butter, sour cream, jam, or honey

Matryoshki (dolls) vegetable salad. The eggs are topped with red and black caviar "hair styles" and wrapped in tiny cloth scarfs.

that are used as toppings, making them juicy and delicious.

Pies are another traditional Russian national dish. Russian pies are comparatively small, elongated, and consist of a filling covered with pastry and baked in the oven. The pastry for the pies may be leavened or unleavened, and the fillings may differ to include cabbage, peas, turnips, carrots, potatoes, spring onions, mushrooms, meat, fish, and even *kasha*. One variety of pie is known as *kulebyaka* ("kool-ee-BYAH-kah")—these are large and the filling (meat, mushrooms, onions, or *kasha*) is spread in layers.

There is another large type of pie that covers the entire baking sheet. These pies are open and not covered with pastry (a bit like a pizza), and are filled with jam. They may have pastry latticework on top.

At the end of the meal, you will be served dessert, consisting of coffee or tea (served in a glass) with candies or spice-cakes—buns with honey and spices, covered with sweet syrup. Spice-cakes appeared in Rus sometime around the ninth century, consisting of a mixture of rye flour and honey or the juice of berries. People later began to add spices—cinnamon, cloves, cardamon, and ginger—and this is how the cakes got their name.

Apart from the spice-cakes, you will be offered different jams, which Russian housewives make well. Particularly popular are raspberry, strawberry, apple, and pear jams. Russians often add a spoonful of jam or preserves to their tea instead of using sugar to sweeten the flavor.

Bliny (pancakes) surrounded by a number of possible toppings, including caviar, sour cream, jam, and honey.

DRINKS

The national Russian beverages are *kvass* ("kvahs") and *mors* ("morhs"). *Kvass* is a beverage that resembles beer, only without the bitterness and alcohol; it is made from fermented yeast, sugar, and fruit and berry juices. *Mors* is made of berry juice diluted with water and slightly fermented.

In times past, there were many meads (alcoholic drinks fermented from honey and water), but they have since disappeared due to the difficulty of making them.

Of the strong liquors, Russian vodka is known the world over. It is a very potent (40% proof) alcoholic drink.

Vodka is the most popular drink for toasting any celebration in Russia.

CUISINE OF THE TATARS AND VOLGA PEOPLES

The dishes of these people are in many respects similar to those of central Asian, and especially Uzbek, cuisine. Typical of this style of cooking are soups of the *shurpa* ("shor-PAH") type—made from vegetables, cereals, and fat mutton. *Shurpa* is prepared with a lot of onions, as well as spices—pepper, coriander, and bay leaf. Also very popular is a soup made with *katyk* ("kah-TIHK"), which is a sour milk made from boiled milk.

Specific to Tatar cuisine are dishes made from horsemeat that has been boiled, dried, and cured. The best-known of the dessert candies is *chak-chak* ("chak chak"), which are pieces of pastry boiled in honey.

A "cowboy" of the tundra ropes in a reindeer. The people of the northern wastes often eat raw reindeer meat.

CUISINE OF THE CAUCASUS

The food of this region is something of a mixture of the central Asian, Georgian, and Azerbaijani cuisines. From the Turks and central Asians the unleavened flat cakes are borrowed, plus dishes made from mutton, and soups of the *shurpa* style. From the Georgians come *shashlyks* and brine cheeses, and from the Azerbaijanis, *khalva* ("HAHL-vah"), a sweet made from nuts and sunflower seeds. The most typical dish of the region is *khinkal* ("kin-KAHL")—thick noodles boiled with mutton and spices, and *chudu* (choo-DOO")—fried pies of meat, cottage cheese, and onion fillings.

CUISINE OF THE NORTH

This cuisine is the most exotic and unusual. In Arctic conditions, the people have devised a special menu consisting of raw meat and fish. For a long time this was considered a sign of barbarity and savagery, but then it was discovered that the people in northern Russia never suffered from beriberi and other vitamin deficiencies, unlike other Russians. It has also been scientifically proven that their cuisine is ideal for arctic conditions.

Raw food can be of three kinds: fresh meat and fish; the fat and blood of an animal (reindeer, seal, or whale); and both frozen together. *Stroganina* ("Strog-ah-NIN-ah") is a dish that consists of finely sliced meat or fish that is immediately eaten spiced with salt, roots, and berries, and wind-dried meat and fish. Naturally, northern people also like hot dishes—tea, tea with milk, and hot drinks and products made from reindeer milk.

CABBAGE PIE

Ingredients for pastry:
1 lb flour
1 cup sour cream
2 tablespoons butter or margarine
1 tablespoon sugar
½ teaspoon salt
2 eggs
egg white, beaten lightly with a fork

If you have no sour cream, dough can instead be made from the following ingredients:
1 lb flour
4 oz butter or margarine
1 tablespoon sugar
2 tablespoons vodka or brandy
½ teaspoon

The dough made from this quantity will be enough for 20–25 pies.

Method:
Sift the flour, make a well in the center, and add the sour cream, butter, salt, and sugar. Beat the eggs and quickly mix ingredients into a dough. Shape into a ball and refrigerate the dough for 30–40 minutes. Roll it out to ⅕ of an inch thick, cut circles with a glass or cup, and put some filling in the center of each circle. Fold the dough over, then pinch the edges to seal. Glaze the top with beaten egg white. Put the pies on a baking sheet and bake in the oven at medium-high heat for 15–20 minutes. To check whether the pies are cooked, pierce one with a toothpick—if the dough does not stick to the toothpick, the pie is ready. The pies should be golden.

Ingredients for filling:
1 head of cabbage
2–3 tablespoons butter
3–4 hardboiled eggs, chopped
salt
sugar

Method:
Clean and chop the cabbage, scald it with boiling water, then drain. Pour cold water on it, drain again thoroughly, and put into a pan with melted butter. Fry for 10 minutes, stirring all the time. Add the chopped hardboiled eggs, salt, and a spoonful of sugar.

ARCTIC OCEAN

A B C D

N

BARENTS SEA

SWEDEN

FINLAND

NEW SIBERIAN ISLANDS

SEVERNAYA ZEMLYA

BALTIC SEA

● Murmansk

NOVAYA ZEMLYA

1

Kaliningrad

ESTONIA

Lake Ladoga

LATVIA

● Pskov

LITHUANIA

● St. Petersburg

● Archangelsk

Oymyakon ●

● Novgorod

Central

BELARUS

● Vologda

Siberian

Kiev

Smolensk

● Yaroslav

West

Lena

2

● Tver

● Kostroma

Plateau

● MOSCOW

● Vladimir

Siberian

Ob

● Yakutsk

● Ryazan

● Kirov

Ural Mountains

● Nizhniy
Novgorod

● Kazan

Plain

Yenisey

UKRAINE

Volga

● Perm

● Ulyanovsk

● Yekaterinburg

Angara

● Saratov

● Samara

Don

● Magnitogorsk

● Chelyabinsk

Rostov-
on-Don ●

Lake
Baikal

● Volgograd

● Omsk

● Tomsk

Mt. Elbrus
(18,465ft.) ▲

● Astrakhan

● Novosibirsk

● Krasnovarsk

3

GEORGIA

Caucasus

CASPIAN SEA

KAZAKHSTAN

● Chita

● Irkutsk

ARMENIA

● Ulan Ude

AZERBAIJAN

MONGOLIA

UZBEKISTAN

TURKMENISTAN

KYRGYZSTAN

4

TAJIKISTAN

CHINA

RUSSIA

Map legend:
- ● Capital city
- ● Major town
- ▲ Mountain peak

Height of land (feet)
- over 9000
- 6000 – 9000
- 3000 – 6000
- 1500 – 3000
- 600 – 1500
- 0 – 600

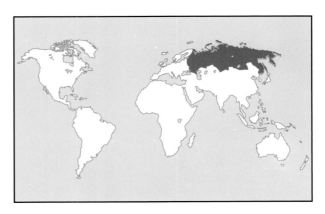

QUICK NOTES

LAND AREA
6.6 million square miles

POPULATION
148.7 million

CAPITAL
Moscow

MAIN RIVERS
Ob (with Irtysh)—3,354 miles
Amur (with tributaries)—2,737 miles
Lena—2,800 miles
Yenisey—2,566 miles
Volga—2,325 miles
Don—1,200 miles

MAIN LAKES AND SEAS
Caspian Sea—169,000 square miles
Baikal (the world's deepest lake—5,714 feet)—13,200 square miles
Ladoga—7,000 square miles
Onega—3,764 square miles

MOUNTAIN RANGES
The Urals
Altai
Caucasus
Verkhoyansk Range (Siberia)
Cherski Range (Siberia)
Stanovoi Range (Siberia)

MAIN PEAKS
Elbrus (Caucasus)—18,465 feet
Klyuchevskaya Sopka (Kamchatka)—15,548 feet
Belukha (Altai)—14,869 feet

LANGUAGE
Russian

CURRENCY
The ruble—$1 = 1,300 rubles (January 1994)

IMPORTANT LEADERS
Ivan IV (1530–1584)—First formally proclaimed tsar of Russia, in 1547. Known as "Ivan the Terrible" because of the brutality of his reign.

Peter I (1672–1725)—Tsar from 1696–1725, and probably the most outstanding reformer in Russian history. He modernized Russia and drew it into the European sphere.

Catherine II (1729–1796)—Empress from 1762 to 1796. Following Peter I, she led her country into full participation in the political and cultural life of Europe.

Vladimir Ilyich Lenin (1870–1924)—Founder of the Russian Communist Party and leader of the 1917 Bolshevik Revolution, he was the first head of the new Soviet state (1917–1924).

GLOSSARY

Cyrillic alphabet A written system developed in the ninth century for Slavic peoples of the Eastern Orthodox faith. Based on the Greek script of the same period, the Cyrillic alphabet was invented by two Greek brothers, Cyril (from where the script derives its name) and Methodius.

bliny ("BLEE-nee") A light, porous, fluffy pancake. Preparation requires the minimum of flour and the maximum of water or milk.

Duma Meaning assembly or council, the first Duma was initiated as a result of the failed 1905 Revolution. The *Duma* was a state assembly that constituted the state legislature from 1906 until its dissolution in 1917.

glasnost ("GLAHZ-nost") Literally means "openness." Former USSR president Mikhail Gorbachev's declared public policy of openly discussing economic and political realities.

kasha ("KAH-shah") A similiquid dish made from a variety of cereals.

Oprichnina ("ah-PRICH-ni-na") A policy of terror under Ivan IV. Ivan divided his territory into two parts, one to be ruled in the traditional manner, and the second—referred to as the widow's part (*oprich*)—he ruled personally, aided by a loyal and brutal bodyguard of 5,000 men.

perestroika ("peh-reh-STROI-kah") Literally means "rebuilding." The program of political and economic reform in the USSR initiated by Mikhail Gorbachev in 1986.

serfdom A modified form of slavery whereby peasants were bound by oath to an hereditary plot of land and to a landowner. The landowner, in effect, owned the peasants and could buy and sell them as he pleased, or volunteer them for army service. Serfdom was abolished in Russia by Tsar Alexander II in 1861.

steppes An extensive plain, usually bare and inhospitable.

taiga ("TAI-gah") Coniferous evergreen forests of subarctic lands covering vast tracts of Russia, especially in Siberia.

Zemstvo Elected rural councils first established in 1864 to provide social and economic services. They introduced schools for the common people, supervised road construction, and provided some health care.

BIBLIOGRAPHY

Fodor's Russia: the Republics and the Baltics, Fodor's Travel Publications, New York, 1991.

Hughes, Gwyneth: *Red Empire: The Forbidden History of the USSR*, St. Martin's Press, New York, 1990.

Kempe, Frederick: *Siberian Odyssey: A Voyage into the Russian Soul*, G.P. Putnam's Sons, New York, 1992.

Pasternak, Boris: *Doctor Zhivago*, 1957.

Tolstoy, Leo: *War and Peace*, 1863–6.

INDEX

INDEX

INDEX

PICTURE CREDITS